PRENTICE HALL
Realidades ①

Practice Workbook with Writing, Audio & Video Activities

PEARSON
Prentice
Hall

Boston, Massachusetts
Upper Saddle River, New Jersey

ISBN 0-13-116463-5

30 31 32 33 34 35 36 V0N4 17 16 15 14

Practice Workbook

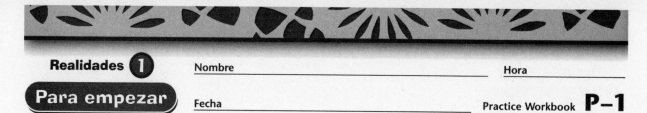

Realidades **1**

Para empezar

En la escuela

Nombre _____

Fecha _____

Hora _____

Practice Workbook **P–1**

¿Cómo te llamas?

It is the first day of school in Madrid, and students are getting to know each other. Complete the dialogues by circling the appropriate words and phrases.

1. **A:** ¡Hola! (Hasta luego. / ¿Cómo te llamas?)

   B: Me llamo Rubén. ¿Y tú?

   A: Me llamo Antonio.

   B: (Mucho gusto. / Bien, gracias.)

   A: Igualmente, Rubén.

2. It is 9:00 in the morning.

   A: (¡Buenas tardes! / ¡Buenos días!) ¿Cómo te llamas?

   B: Buenos días. Me llamo Rosalía. ¿Cómo te llamas tú?

   A: Me llamo Enrique. (¿Cómo estás, Rosalía? / Gracias, Rosalía.)

   B: Muy bien, gracias. ¿Y tú?

   A: (Encantado. / Bien.)

   B: Adiós, Enrique.

   A: (¡Sí! / ¡Nos vemos!)

3. It is now 2:00 P.M.

   A: ¡Buenas tardes, Sr. Gómez!

   B: (¡Buenas noches! / ¡Buenas tardes!) ¿Cómo te llamas?

   A: Me llamo Margarita.

   B: Mucho gusto, Margarita.

   A: (Buenos días. / Encantada.) ¡Adiós, Sr. Gómez!

   B: (¡Hasta luego! / ¡Bien!)

¿Eres formal o informal?

A. Circle the phrases below that can be used to talk to teachers. Underline the phrases that can be used to talk to other students. Some phrases may be both circled and underlined.

¡Hola!	¿Cómo está Ud.?	Mucho gusto.	¿Qué tal?
Buenos días.	¿Cómo estás?	¿Y usted?	¡Hasta luego!
¡Nos vemos!	Buenos días, señor.	Estoy bien.	¿Y tú?

B. Circle **Ud.** or **tú** to indicate how you would address the person being spoken to.

1. "Hola, Sr. Gómez."   **Ud.**   **Tú**

2. "¿Qué tal, Luis?"   **Ud.**   **Tú**

3. "¿Cómo estás, Paco?"   **Ud.**   **Tú**

4. "¡Buenos días, profesor!"   **Ud.**   **Tú**

5. "Adiós, señora."   **Ud.**   **Tú**

C. Number the following phrases from 1–5 to create a logical conversation. Number 1 should indicate the first thing that was said, and 5 should indicate the last thing that was said.

_____ Bien, gracias, ¿y Ud.?

_____ ¡Hasta luego!

_____ Buenas tardes.

_____ ¡Buenas tardes! ¿Cómo está Ud.?

_____ Muy bien. ¡Adiós!

Realidades ❶

Para empezar

En la escuela

Nombre _____

Fecha _____

Hora _____

Practice Workbook **P–3**

Por favor

Your Spanish teacher has asked you to learn some basic classroom commands. Write the letter of the appropriate phrase next to the picture it corresponds to.

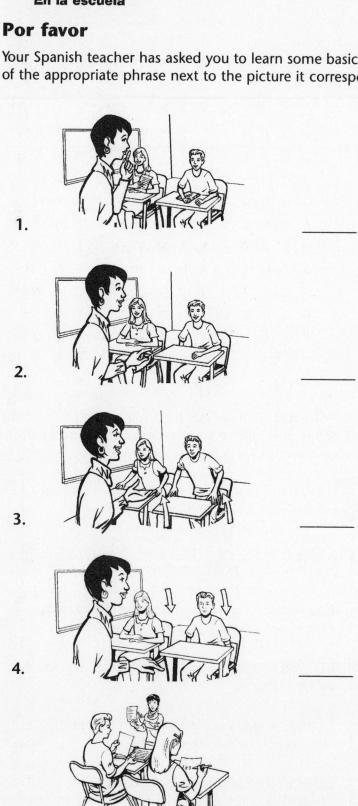

1. _____

2. _____

3. _____

4. _____

5. _____

A. Saquen una hoja de papel.

B. Siéntense, por favor.

C. Repitan, por favor.

D. ¡Silencio, por favor!

E. Levántense, por favor.

Realidades ①

Para empezar

En la escuela

Nombre _____

Fecha _____

Hora _____

Practice Workbook **P–4**

Los números

A. Here are some simple math problems. First, fill in each blank with the correct number. Then, find the Spanish word for that number in the word search to the right.

1. $7 \times 8 =$ _____

2. $50, 40,$ _____ $, 20, 10 \ldots$

3. $75 + 7 =$ _____

4. $55, 60, 65,$ _____ $, 75, 80 \ldots$

5. $97, 98, 99,$ _____ $\ldots$

6. $24 \div 2 =$ _____

7. $72, 60,$ _____ $, 36, 24 \ldots$

```
O C H E N T A Y D O S L C T
M O J X U E Y S W H U S S R
O G X L E G I L E C E H M E
G U N V C T B C R T U C G I
O H C O Y A T N E R A U C N
T T C C V A T N W L Y F W T
M B K W C E T U Y O N L O A
E F Q F Q A N B Y F K R L V
H C E E A Y R T D M W D A W
C I N C U E N T A Y S E I S
R E C O J I W C J Y G Q U Q
U L J D I U D G V X D D K G
```

B. As exchange students, you and your classmates are finding it hard to get used to the time difference. Below are some statements about time differences in various U.S and Spanish-speaking cities. Write in the times that correspond to each. Follow the model.

Modelo	`10:30` `10:30`	Cuando son las diez y media en Chicago, son las diez y media en Panamá.
1.	`:` `:`	Cuando es la una y media en Washington, D.C., son las dos y media en Buenos Aires.
2.	`:` `:`	Cuando son las doce y cuarto en Ciudad de México, es la una y cuarto en San Juan.
3.	`:` `:`	Cuando son las diez en Nueva York, son las diez en La Habana.
4.	`:` `:`	Cuando son las seis y cuarto en San Francisco, son las ocho y cuarto en Lima.
5.	`:` `:`	Cuando son las dos de la mañana (*A.M.*) en Madrid, son las siete de la tarde (*P.M.*) en Bogotá.

Go Online WEB CODE jcd-0002
PHSchool.com

Realidades ①

Para empezar

En la escuela

Nombre _____

Hora _____

Fecha _____

Practice Workbook **P–5**

El cuerpo

A. You are watching your neighbor's toddler Anita for a few hours after school. She is playing with her **muñequita** (*doll*) Chula and is practicing words to identify body parts. Help her by drawing lines to connect her doll's body parts with their correct names.

el ojo

la boca

el dedo

el estómago

la nariz

la mano

el brazo

el pie

la cabeza

la pierna

B. Now write three sentences using the phrase **me duele** and body parts.

1. _____

2. _____

3. _____

Realidades **1**

Para empezar

En la clase

Nombre _____

Fecha _____

Hora _____

Practice Workbook **P–6**

Combinaciones

A. Write the correct article (**el** or **la**, or both) before each of the items below.

1. _____ bolígrafo

2. _____ lápiz

3. _____ sala de clases

4. _____ profesora

5. _____ cuaderno

6. _____ carpeta

7. _____ profesor

8. _____ estudiante

9. _____ pupitre

10. _____ hoja de papel

B. To make sure that there are enough school supplies for everyone, your teacher has asked you to help take inventory. Complete each sentence by writing the name and number of each item pictured. Follow the model.

Modelo   veinticinco   No hay un *libro* . Hay *25* _____.

1.   sesenta y siete   No hay un _____ . Hay _____.

2.   cien   No hay una _____ . Hay _____.

3.   veintidos   No hay un _____ . Hay _____.

4.   diecinueve   No hay un _____ . Hay _____.

5.   treinta y seis   No hay un _____ . Hay _____.

Go Online WEB CODE jcd-0004
PHSchool.com

Realidades ❶

Para empezar

En la clase

Nombre _____

Hora _____

Fecha _____

Practice Workbook **P–7**

El calendario

February has just ended on a leap year. Because of this, Pepe is completely lost in planning out March. Help him get his days straight by using the calendar. Follow the model.

lunes	martes	miércoles	jueves	viernes	sábado	domingo
				1	2	3
4	5	6	7	8	9	10
11	12	13	14	15	16	17
18	19	20	21	22	23	24
25	26	27	28	29	30	31

Modelo TÚ: Hoy es el cinco de marzo.

PEPE: ¿Es jueves?

TÚ: No, es martes.

1. TÚ: Hoy es el treinta de marzo.

PEPE: ¿Es lunes?

TÚ: _____

2. TÚ: Hoy es el trece de marzo.

PEPE: ¿Es domingo?

TÚ: _____

3. TÚ: Hoy es el veintiuno de marzo.

PEPE: ¿Es domingo?

TÚ: _____

4. TÚ: Hoy es el once de marzo.

PEPE: ¿Es miércoles?

TÚ: _____

5. TÚ: Hoy es el primero de marzo.

PEPE: ¿Es martes?

TÚ: _____

6. TÚ: Hoy es el doce de marzo.

PEPE: ¿Es sábado?

TÚ: _____

7. TÚ: Hoy es el veinticuatro de marzo.

PEPE: ¿Es viernes?

TÚ: _____

8. TÚ: Hoy es el diecisiete de marzo.

PEPE: ¿Es lunes?

TÚ: _____

La fecha

A. Write out the following dates in Spanish. The first one is done for you.

Día/Mes

2/12   _el dos de diciembre_____

9/3   _____

5/7   _____

4/9   _____

8/11   _____

1/1   _____

> **¿Recuerdas?**
>
> Remember that when writing the date in Spanish, the day precedes the month.
>
> - 19/12 = el 19 de diciembre = December 19
> - 27/3 = el 27 de marzo = March 27

B. Now, answer the following questions about dates in complete sentences.

1. ¿Cuál es la fecha de hoy?

_____

2. ¿El Día de San Valentín es el trece de enero?

_____

3. ¿Cuál es la fecha del Año Nuevo?

_____

4. ¿La Navidad (*Christmas*) es el 25 de noviembre?

_____

5. ¿Cuál es la fecha del Día de San Patricio?

_____

6. ¿Cuál es la fecha del Día de la Independencia?

_____

7. ¿Cuál es la fecha de mañana?

_____

¿Qué tiempo hace?

You and several Spanish-speaking exchange students are discussing the weather of your home countries.

A. Fill in the chart with the missing information for the area in which you live.

Meses	Estación	Tiempo
diciembre enero _____	_____	_____
marzo _____ _____	_____	_____
junio _____ _____	verano	_____
_____ _____ noviembre	_____	hace viento, hace sol

B. Complete the dialogues below with information from the chart.

1. PROFESORA: ¿Qué tiempo hace en julio?

   ESTUDIANTE: _____

2. PROFESORA: ¿En enero hace calor?

   ESTUDIANTE: _____

3. PROFESORA: ¿En qué meses hace frío?

   ESTUDIANTE: _____

4. PROFESORA: ¿Qué tiempo hace en el verano?

   ESTUDIANTE: _____

5. PROFESORA: ¿Nieva en agosto?

   ESTUDIANTE: _____

Realidades ❶

Para empezar

Nombre _____

Fecha _____

Hora _____

Practice Workbook **P–10**

Repaso

Fill in the crossword puzzle with the Spanish translation of the English words given below.

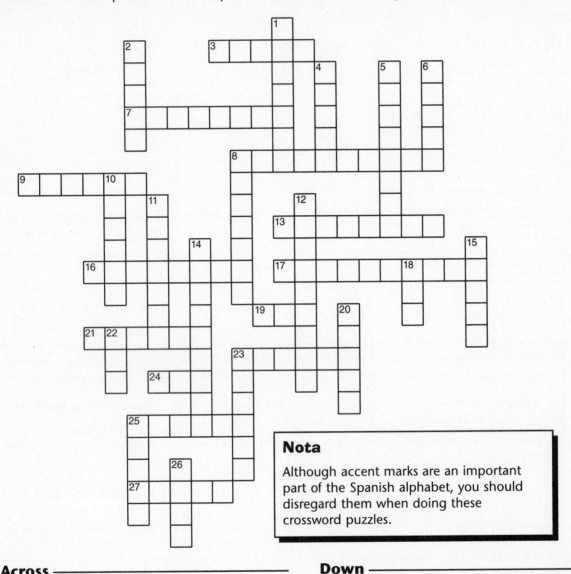

Nota

Although accent marks are an important part of the Spanish alphabet, you should disregard them when doing these crossword puzzles.

Across

3. pencil
7. season
8. See you later!
9. it is raining
13. it is cold
16. winter
17. September
19. day
21. head
23. madam, Mrs.
24. foot
25. week
27. fall

Down

1. Friday
2. Monday
4. it is snowing
5. male teacher
6. January
8. it is sunny
10. summer
11. desk
12. it is hot
14. spring
15. the date
18. month
20. arm
22. year
23. Saturday
25. sir, Mr.
26. Hello

Realidades 1

Para empezar

Nombre _____

Hora _____

Fecha _____

Practice Workbook **P–11**

Organizer

I. Vocabulary

Greetings and good-byes

_____

_____

_____

_____

_____

Classroom objects

_____

_____

_____

_____

_____

Body parts

_____

_____

_____

_____

_____

_____

_____

Words to talk about time

_____

_____

_____

_____

Phrases to talk about names

_____

_____

Forms of address (Formal)

_____

_____

Forms of address (Informal)

_____

Phrases to ask and tell how you feel

_____

_____

_____

_____

Realidades ①

Para empezar

Nombre _____

Fecha _____

Hora _____

Practice Workbook **P–11**

Days of the week

_____
_____
_____
_____
_____
_____

Months of the year

_____
_____
_____
_____
_____
_____
_____
_____
_____
_____

Seasons

_____
_____
_____
_____

Weather expressions

_____
_____
_____

II. Grammar

1. The word *the* is a definite article in English. The singular definite articles in Spanish are _____ and _____ , as in _____ **libro** and _____ **carpeta**.

2. Most nouns ending with _____ are masculine. Most nouns ending with _____ are feminine.

Go Online WEB CODE jcd-0007
PHSchool.com

Realidades 1

Capítulo 1A

Nombre _____

Fecha _____

Hora _____

Practice Workbook **1A–1**

La pregunta perfecta

Complete each sentence using the word or phrase that best describes the picture.

1.  ¿Te gusta _____?

2.  A mí me gusta _____.

3.  ¿Te gusta _____?

4.  No me gusta _____. ¿Y a ti?

5.   Pues, me gusta mucho _____.

6.  Sí, me gusta mucho _____.

7.  ¿Te gusta mucho _____?

8.  Me gusta _____.

9.  ¡Me gusta mucho _____!

10.  No, ¡no me gusta nada _____!

Realidades 1

Capítulo 1A

Nombre _____

Fecha _____

Hora _____

Practice Workbook **1A–2**

¿A ti también?

Several friends are talking at the bus stop about what they like and do not like to do. Based on the pictures, write the activity that the first person likes or does not like to do. Then, complete the second person's response. Make sure to use **también** or **tampoco** when expressing agreement and disagreement.

1.

ENRIQUE: A mí me gusta mucho _____.
¿A ti te gusta?

DOLORES: Sí, _____.

2.

PABLO: Me gusta _____.
¿A ti te gusta?

MARTA: No, _____.

3.

JAIME: No me gusta _____.
¿A ti te gusta?

JULIO: No, _____.

4.

MARÍA: Me gusta _____.
¿A ti te gusta?

JULIA: No _____.

5.

CARMEN: No me gusta nada _____.
¿A ti te gusta?

JOSEFINA: Sí, _____.

6.

ROBERTO: Me gusta _____.
¿A ti te gusta?

PEDRO: Sí, _____.

Go Online
PHSchool.com

WEB CODE
jcd-0101

Realidades ❶

Capítulo 1A

Nombre _____

Hora _____

Fecha _____

Practice Workbook **1A–3**

¿Te gusta o no te gusta?

You are talking to some new students about the things that they like to do. Using the drawings and the model below, complete the following mini-conversations.

Modelo

☺

—¿Te gusta _hablar por teléfono_?
—_Sí, me gusta mucho._

☹

—¿Te gusta _nadar_?
—_No, no me gusta nada._

☹

1. —¿Te gusta _____?

   _____ .

☺

2. —¿Te gusta _____?

   _____ .

☺

3. —¿Te gusta _____?

   _____ .

☹

4. —¿Te gusta _____?

   _____ .

☺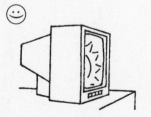

5. —¿Te gusta _____?

   _____ .

☺

6. —¿Te gusta _____?

   _____ .

Realidades ❶

Capítulo 1A

Nombre _____

Fecha _____

Hora _____

Practice Workbook **1A–4**

¿Qué te gusta hacer?

Complete the dialogues below to find out what activities these friends like and dislike.

1. MIGUEL: ¿Te gusta ir a la escuela?

   RITA: Sí. _____ mucho ir a la escuela.

   ¿Y _____?

   MIGUEL: Sí, a mí me gusta _____ también. No me gusta

   _____ ver la tele _____ jugar videojuegos.

   RITA: _____ tampoco.

2. JUAN: No _____ patinar.

   PAULA: _____ tampoco. Me gusta leer revistas.

   JUAN: ¿_____ más, trabajar o

   _____?

   PAULA: _____ hablar por teléfono.

   JUAN: Sí. A mí _____ .

3. AMELIA: A mí _____ pasar tiempo con mis amigos.

   CARLOS: A mí me gusta _____ también.

   AMELIA: ¿Te gusta trabajar?

   CARLOS: No, _____ .

   AMELIA: _____ tampoco.

Go Online WEB CODE jcd-0102
PHSchool.com

El infinitivo

Decide what infinitive each picture represents. Then, based on its ending, write the verb in the appropriate column. Use the model as a guide.

	-ar	-er	-ir
Modelo	patinar		
1.			
2.			
3.			
4.			
5.			
6.			
7.			
8.			

Realidades **1**

Capítulo 1A

Nombre _____

Hora _____

Fecha _____

Practice Workbook **1A–6**

Las actividades en común

Cristina is feeling very negative. Using the pictures to help you, write Cristina's negative responses to Lola's questions. Use the model to help you.

Modelo

LOLA: _¿Te gusta patinar?_ _____

CRISTINA: _No, no me gusta nada patinar._ _____

1. LOLA: _____

    CRISTINA: _____

2. LOLA: _____

    CRISTINA: _____

3. LOLA: _____

    CRISTINA: _____

4. LOLA: _____

    CRISTINA: _____

5. LOLA: _____

    CRISTINA: _____

Go Online WEB CODE jcd-0104
PHSchool.com

Realidades 1

Capítulo 1A

Nombre _____

Hora _____

Fecha _____

Practice Workbook **1A–7**

La conversación completa

At lunch, you overhear a conversation between Sara and Graciela, who are trying to decide what they would like to do after school today. Since it is noisy in the cafeteria, you miss some of what they say. Read the conversation through to get the gist, then fill in the missing lines with what the friends probably said.

GRACIELA: ¿Qué te gusta hacer?

SARA: _____ .

GRACIELA: ¿Nadar? Pero es el invierno. ¡Hace frío!

SARA: Sí. Pues, también _____ .

GRACIELA: Pero hoy es martes y no hay programas buenos en la tele.

SARA: Pues, ¿qué _____ hacer a ti?

GRACIELA: _____ .

SARA: ¡Uf! Hay un problema. No me gusta ni jugar videojuegos ni usar la computadora.

GRACIELA: Hmm . . . ¿_____?

SARA: No, _____ nada patinar.

GRACIELA: ¿Te gusta bailar o cantar?

SARA: No, _____ .

GRACIELA: Pues, ¿qué _____ , Sara?

SARA: _____ hablar por teléfono.

GRACIELA: ¡A mí también! ¿Cuál es tu número de teléfono?

Realidades 1

Capítulo 1A

Nombre _____

Fecha _____

Hora _____

Practice Workbook **1A–8**

Repaso

Fill in the crossword puzzle below with the actions indicated by the pictures.

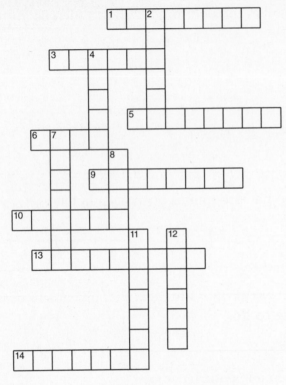

Down

2.

4.

7.

8.

11.

12.

Across

1.

3.

5.

6.

9.

10.

13.

14.

Organizer

I. Vocabulary

Activities I like to do

_____

_____

_____

_____

_____

Activities I may not like to do

_____

_____

_____

_____

_____

Words to say what I like to do

_____

_____

_____

Words to say what I don't like to do

_____

_____

_____

Words to ask what others like to do

_____

_____

_____

_____

II. Grammar

1. The infinitive in English is expressed by writing the word _____ before a verb. In Spanish the infinitive is expressed by the verb endings _____ , _____ , and _____ .

2. In order to say that something doesn't happen in Spanish, use the word _____ before the verb.

3. Use the word _____ to agree with someone who likes something. Use the word _____ to agree with someone who dislikes something.

4. If you do not like either of two choices, use the word _____ .

Realidades 1

Capítulo 1B

Nombre _____

Fecha _____

Hora _____

Practice Workbook **1B–1**

¿Cómo es?

At school you see many different types of people. Describe each person you see in the picture by writing the appropriate adjective on the corresponding blank.

1. _____

2. _____

3. _____

4. _____

5. _____

6. _____

7. _____

8. _____

Go Online WEB CODE jcd-0111
PHSchool.com

Realidades 1

Capítulo 1B

Nombre _____

Hora _____

Fecha _____

Practice Workbook **1B–2**

Un juego de descripción

Each picture below represents a personality trait. Unscramble the word to identify each trait. Write down the trait, and then circle the picture that corresponds to the unscrambled word.

1. ísiattcar _____

2. rvoidate _____

3. ddonaesdreo _____

4. jadartobaar _____

5. iacoarsg _____

6. zeerosap _____

7. vesrdoaer _____

8. utoiesdas _____

Realidades ①

Nombre _____

Hora _____

Capítulo 1B

Fecha _____

Practice Workbook **1B–3**

¿Cómo eres?

Tito is interviewing Jorge and Ana, two new students from Costa Rica. Tito's questions are written below, but most of Jorge's and Ana's answers are missing. Complete their answers, using the model to help you.

Modelo TITO: Ana, ¿eres perezosa?

ANA: No, *no soy perezosa* _____.

1. TITO: Jorge, ¿eres talentoso?

   JORGE: Sí, _____.

2. TITO: Ana, ¿eres estudiosa?

   ANA: Sí, _____.

3. TITO: Jorge, ¿eres desordenado?

   JORGE: No, _____.

4. TITO: Ana, ¿eres deportista?

   ANA: No, _____.

5. TITO: Jorge, ¿eres sociable?

   JORGE: Sí, _____.

6. TITO: Ana, ¿eres paciente?

   ANA: No, _____.

7. TITO: Jorge, ¿eres inteligente?

   JORGE: Sí, _____.

8. TITO: Ana, ¿eres artística?

   ANA: No, _____.

Go Online WEB CODE jcd-0112
PHSchool.com

Realidades ❶

Capítulo 1B

Nombre _____

Hora _____

Fecha _____

Practice Workbook **1B–4**

¿Qué les gusta?

Based on what each person likes to do, write a description of him or her. Follow the model.

Modelo   A Roberto le gusta esquiar.

Roberto es atrevido. _____

1. A Esteban le gusta tocar la guitarra.

    _____

2. A Pedro le gusta hablar por teléfono.

    _____

3. A Claudia le gusta practicar deportes.

    _____

4. A Teresa le gusta estudiar.

    _____

5. A Luz no le gusta trabajar.

    _____

6. A Manuela le gusta ir a la escuela.

    _____

7. A Carmen le gusta pasar tiempo con amigos.

    _____

8. A Lucía le gusta dibujar.

    _____

Realidades ①

Capítulo 1B

Nombre _____

Fecha _____

Hora _____

Practice Workbook **1B–5**

Me gusta . . .

Some new exchange students at your school are introducing themselves. Using the model as a guide, fill in the blanks in their statements with the actions and adjectives suggested by the pictures. Do not forget to use the correct (masculine or feminine) form of the adjective.

Modelo

A mí _me gusta leer_____.

Yo _soy inteligente_____.

1.

A mí _____.

Yo _____.

2.

A mí _____.

Yo _____.

3.

A mí _____.

Yo _____.

4.

A mí _____.

Yo _____.

5.

A mí _____.

Yo _____.

6.

A mí _____.

Yo _____.

Go Online WEB CODE jcd-0114
PHSchool.com

¿Un o una?

A. Look at the drawings below and decide if they represent masculine or feminine words. Then, label the item in the space provided. Don't forget to use the appropriate indefinite article (**un** or **una**).

Modelo _un profesor_

1. _____

2. _____

3. _____

4. _____

5. _____

6. _____

B. Now, look at the drawings below and describe each person. Make sure to use all the words from the word bank. Don't forget to use the correct definite article (**el** or **la**) and to make the adjectives agree with the nouns.

| estudiante | familia | chico | chica | profesor | profesora |

Modelo _La estudiante_
es trabajadora.

1. _____

2. _____

3. _____

4. _____

5. _____

6. _____

Realidades ①

Capítulo 1B

Nombre _____

Fecha _____

Hora _____

Practice Workbook **1B–7**

Oraciones completas

Choose sentence parts from each of the word banks below, then put them in the correct order to form complete sentences. Follow the model.

Subjects:		Verbs:	
Marta	Yo	es soy eres	
El Sr. Brown	Rolando		
La Srta. Moloy	Tú		
Indefinite articles + nouns:		**Adjectives:**	
un estudiante	una estudiante	reservado(a)	deportista
un chico	un profesor	inteligente	estudioso(a)
una chica	una profesora	perezoso(a)	bueno(a)

Modelo   *Yo soy un chico estudioso.* _____

1. _____

2. _____

3. _____

4. _____

5. _____

6. _____

7. _____

8. _____

9. _____

10. _____

Go Online WEB CODE jcd-0115
PHSchool.com

Realidades 1

Capítulo 1B

Nombre _____

Hora _____

Fecha _____

Practice Workbook **1B-8**

Repaso

Down ―――――――――――――

1. según mi ____
2. no paciente
3. no ordenado
5. Un chico/una chica que practica deportes es ____.
6. *I like: "Me ____."*

8.

11. No es trabajador. Es ____.

13.

15.

16. Le gusta pasar tiempo con amigos. Es ____.

18. —¿Cómo ____?
    —Soy sociable.

Across ―――――――――――――

4.

7. *nice, friendly*

9. no es malo, es ____

10. ¿ ____ se llama?

12.

14.

17.

19.

20.

Repaso del capítulo ― *Crucigrama* **29**

Organizer

I. Vocabulary

Words that describe me

_____

_____

_____

_____

_____

Words that may describe others

_____

_____

_____

_____

_____

Words to ask what someone is like

_____

_____

_____

Words to tell what I am like

_____

_____

_____

II. Grammar

1. Most feminine adjectives end with the letter _____. Most masculine adjectives end with the letter _____.

2. Adjectives that can be either masculine or feminine may end with the letters _____ (as in the word _____) or the letter _____ (as in the word _____).

3. The two singular definite articles are _____ and _____. The two singular indefinite articles are _____ and _____.

4. In Spanish, adjectives come (before/after) the nouns they describe.

Go Online WEB CODE jcd-0117
PHSchool.com

Las clases

A. Write the name of the item, and the school subject for which you might use it, in the appropriate column below.

¿Qué es? **¿Para qué clase?**

1. _____ 1. _____

2. _____ 2. _____

3. _____ 3. _____

4. _____ 4. _____

5. _____ 5. _____

6. _____ 6. _____

B. Now, unscramble the letters in each word below to find out what classes you have today and what you need to bring to school.

1. éilsgn: la clase de _____

2. trea: la clase de _____

3. ncoridcoiia: el _____

4. zlpiá: el _____

5. aduclcralao: la

_____

6. ngtíalceoo: la clase de _____

7. birol: el _____

8. lpsñoea: la clase de _____

9. cámtmeistaa: la clase de _____

10. rteaa: la _____

Realidades ❶

Capítulo 2A

Nombre _____

Fecha _____

Hora _____

Practice Workbook **2A–2**

El horario

You have just received your class schedule. Using the model as a guide, write sentences to describe which classes you have and when you have them.

Horario

Hora	Clase
1	inglés
2	matemáticas
3	arte
4	ciencias sociales
5	el almuerzo
6	tecnología
7	español
8	educación física
9	ciencias naturales

Modelo Tengo _la clase de inglés_ en _la primera hora_ .

1. Tengo _____ en _____ .

2. Tengo _____ en _____ .

3. Tengo _____ en _____ .

4. Tengo _____ en _____ .

5. Tengo _____ en _____ .

6. Tengo _____ en _____ .

7. Tengo _____ en _____ .

8. Tengo _____ en _____ .

Go Online WEB CODE jcd-0201
PHSchool.com

¿Cómo son las clases?

Your friend Marcos is curious about which classes you like and which ones you don't like. Answer his questions using adjectives that you have learned in this chapter. Follow the model.

Modelo   ¿Te gusta la clase de matemáticas?

Sí, <u>es interesante</u> .

1. —¿Te gusta la clase de tecnología?

   —Sí, _____ .

2. —¿Te gusta la clase de español?

   —Sí, _____ .

3. —¿Te gusta la clase de matemáticas?

   —No, _____ .

4. —¿Te gusta la clase de ciencias sociales?

   —Sí, _____ .

5. —¿Te gusta la clase de ciencias naturales?

   —No, _____ .

6. —¿Te gusta la clase de educación física?

   —No, _____ .

7. —¿Te gusta la clase de inglés?

   —Sí, _____ .

8. —¿Te gusta la clase de arte?

   —Sí, _____ .

¿Qué necesitas?

You are getting ready for school, and your mother wants to make sure you have everything. Answer her questions according to the model.

Modelo   MAMÁ: ¿Tienes la tarea?
   TÚ: Sí, *tengo la tarea* _____ .

1. MAMÁ: ¿Tienes un libro?

   TÚ: Sí, _____ .

2. MAMÁ: ¿Necesitas una calculadora?

   TÚ: No, _____ .

3. MAMÁ: ¿Tienes una carpeta de argollas para la clase de matemáticas?

   TÚ: No, _____ .

4. MAMÁ: ¿Necesitas un diccionario para la clase de español?

   TÚ: Sí, _____ .

5. MAMÁ: ¿Tienes el cuaderno para la clase de arte?

   TÚ: No, _____ .

6. MAMÁ: ¿Tienes un lápiz?

   TÚ: Sí, _____ .

7. MAMÁ: ¿Necesitas el horario?

   TÚ: No, _____ .

8. MAMÁ: ¿Tienes un bolígrafo?

   TÚ: Sí, _____ .

Go Online WEB CODE jcd-0202
PHSchool.com

Realidades ①

Capítulo 2A

Nombre _____

Hora _____

Fecha _____

Practice Workbook **2A–5**

¡Todo el mundo!

A. How would you talk *about* the following people? Write the correct subject pronoun next to their names. Follow the model.

Modelo   Marisol _____ *ella* _____

1. Pablo _____

2. María y Ester _____

3. Marta y yo _____

4. Tú y Marisol _____

5. El doctor Smith _____

6. Jorge y Tomás _____

7. Carmen _____

8. Alicia y Roberto _____

9. Rolando y Elena _____

B. How would you talk *to* the following people? Write the correct subject pronoun next to their names. Follow the model.

Modelo   Tu amiga Josefina _____ *tú* _____

1. El profesor Santiago _____

2. Marta y Carmen _____

3. Anita y yo _____

4. Tu amigo Federico _____

5. La señorita Ibáñez _____

6. Ricardo _____

7. La profesora Álvarez _____

Realidades ❶

Capítulo 2A

Nombre _____

Fecha _____

Hora _____

Practice Workbook **2A–6**

El verbo exacto

A. Fill in the chart below with all the forms of the verbs given.

	yo	tú	él/ella/Ud.	nosotros/nosotras	vosotros/vosotras	ellos/ellas/Uds.
hablar	hablo				habláis	hablan
estudiar				estudiamos	estudiáis	
enseñar		enseñas			enseñáis	
usar					usáis	
necesitar			necesita		necesitáis	

B. Now, fill in the blanks in the following sentences with the correct forms of the verbs in parentheses.

1. Ella _____ inglés. (estudiar)

2. Yo _____ mucho. (bailar)

3. Nosotros _____ por teléfono. (hablar)

4. Ellos _____ la computadora durante la primera hora. (usar)

5. ¿Quién _____ un bolígrafo? (necesitar)

6. Tú _____ en bicicleta mucho, ¿no? (montar)

7. Uds. _____ muy bien en la clase de arte. (dibujar)

8. Nosotras _____ hoy, ¿no? (patinar)

9. El profesor _____ la lección. (enseñar)

10. Ana y María _____ el libro de español. (necesitar)

11. Jaime _____ todos los días. (caminar)

12. Dolores y yo _____. (bailar)

13. Tú y tus amigos _____ muy bien. (cantar)

¿Qué hacen hoy?

A. Today everyone is doing what he or she likes to do. Follow the model to complete sentences about what everyone is doing.

> **Modelo**   A Luisa le gusta bailar. Hoy _____*ella baila*_____ .

1. A ti te gusta cantar. Hoy _____ .

2. A mí me gusta hablar por teléfono. Hoy _____ .

3. A Francisco le gusta patinar. Hoy _____ .

4. A Ud. le gusta dibujar. Hoy _____ .

5. A Teresa le gusta practicar deportes. Hoy _____ .

B. Using the pictures to help you, tell what everyone is doing today. Follow the model.

Manuel y Carlos

> **Modelo**   Hoy _____*ellos montan en monopatín*_____ .

Amelia y yo

1. Hoy _____ .

tú y Roberto

2. Hoy _____ .

Cristina, Miguel y Linda

3. Hoy _____ .

tú y yo

4. Hoy _____ .

Joaquín y Jaime

5. Hoy _____ .

Sofía y Tomás

6. Hoy _____ .

Realidades (1)

Capítulo 2A

Nombre _____

Hora _____

Fecha _____

Practice Workbook **2A–8**

Repaso

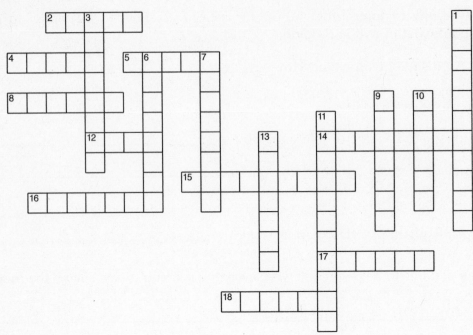

Across

2. No es difícil. Es ____.

4. la ____ de español

5. *homework*

8. educación ____

12. _____ el ____

14. no divertida

15. **ciencias** ____ : *science*

16. ____, octavo, noveno

17. _____ el ____

18. La profesora ____ la clase.

Down

1. _____ la ____

3. ____ **sociales**: *social studies*

6. *lunch*

7. carpeta de ____

9. *schedule*

10. cuarta, ____, sexta

11. _____ la clase de ____

13. primero, segundo, ____

Organizer

I. Vocabulary

Classes I take in school

_____

_____

_____

_____

Words to talk about the order of things

_____

_____

_____

_____

_____

_____

_____

Words used to refer to people

_____

_____

_____

_____

_____

_____

Words to describe my classes

_____

_____

_____

_____

_____

II. Grammar

1. The following are subject pronouns in Spanish: _____, _____,

_____, _____, _____, _____, _____,

_____, _____, _____, _____, _____.

2. Use _____ to address someone formally. Use _____
to address someone informally.

3. The **-ar** verb endings are: _____ _____ _____ _____ _____ _____

Now conjugate the verb **hablar**: _____ _____

_____ _____

_____ _____

En la clase

Label the items in this Spanish class. Make sure to use the correct definite article (**el** or **la**).

1. _____

2. _____   6. _____   10. _____

3. _____   7. _____   11. _____

4. _____   8. _____   12. _____

5. _____   9. _____   13. _____

Go Online WEB CODE jcd-0211
PHSchool.com

¡Mucha confusión!

You come home after school to find a scene of great confusion in your kitchen. Look at the picture, then describe what you see by filling in the blanks in the sentences below with the appropriate words to indicate location.

1. Paquito está _____ del escritorio.

2. Mamá está _____ de la luz (*the light*).

3. Papá está _____ de la ventana.

4. La papelera está _____ de la puerta.

5. Las hojas de papel están _____ de la mesa.

6. Carmen está _____ de la silla.

7. El reloj está _____ de la mesa.

8. El libro está _____ de la silla.

9. El teclado está _____ de la pantalla.

¿Dónde está?

Rosario is describing the room where she studies to a friend of hers on the phone. Using the picture below, write what she might say about where each item is located. There may be more than one right answer. Follow the model.

Modelo   La mochila está _encima de la silla_____.

1. El escritorio está _____.

2. La computadora está _____.

3. La papelera está _____.

4. Los disquetes están _____.

5. Una bandera de los Estados Unidos está _____.

6. La silla está _____.

7. El sacapuntas está _____.

8. Los libros de español están _____.

Go Online WEB CODE jcd-0212
PHSchool.com

¿Qué es esto?

Complete the following conversations that you overhear in school.

1. **A:** ¿_____ estudiantes hay en la clase?

   B: _____ veintidós estudiantes en la clase.

2. **A:** ¿_____?

   B: Es la mochila.

3. **A:** ¿_____ está la computadora?

   B: Está allí, al lado de las ventanas.

4. **A:** ¿_____ una bandera en la sala de clases?

   B: Sí, la bandera está allí.

5. **A:** ¿Dónde están los estudiantes?

   B: Los estudiantes _____ la clase de inglés.

6. **A:** ¿Dónde está el teclado?

   B: Está delante _____ la pantalla.

7. **A:** ¿Dónde está el diccionario?

   B: _____ está, debajo del escritorio.

8. **A:** ¿Qué hay _____ la mochila?

   B: Hay muchos libros.

¿Dónde están?

Spanish teachers are conversing in the faculty room. Fill in their conversations using the correct form of the verb **estar**.

1. —¡Buenos días! ¿Cómo _____ Ud., Sra. López?

   —_____ bien, gracias.

2. —¿Dónde _____ Raúl hoy? No _____ en

   mi clase.

   —¿Raúl? Él _____ en la oficina.

3. —Yo no tengo mis libros. ¿Dónde _____?

   —Sus libros _____ encima de la mesa, profesor Martínez.

4. —¿Cuántos estudiantes _____ aquí?

   —Diecinueve estudiantes _____ aquí. Uno

   no _____ aquí.

5. —¿Dónde _____ mi diccionario?

   —El diccionario _____ detrás del escritorio.

6. —¿Cómo _____ los estudiantes hoy?

   —Teresa _____ bien. Jorge y Bernardo _____

   regulares.

7. —Bien, profesores, ¿_____ nosotros listos (*ready*)? Todos los

   estudiantes _____ en la clase.

Go Online WEB CODE jcd-0214
PHSchool.com

Muchas cosas

A. Fill in the chart below with singular and plural, definite and indefinite forms of the words given. The first word has been completed.

Definite		Indefinite	
singular	plural	singular	plural
la silla	las sillas	una silla	unas sillas
		un cuaderno	
			unos disquetes
	las computadoras		
la mochila			
			unos relojes
		una bandera	
la profesora			

B. Now, fill in each sentence below with words from the chart.

1. Pablo, ¿necesitas _____ de los Estados Unidos? Aquí está.

2. Marta, ¿tienes _____? ¿Qué hora es?

3. Hay _____ Macintosh en la sala de clases.

4. _____ está en la sala de clases. Ella enseña la clase

   de tecnología.

5. Necesito _____ buena. Tengo muchos libros.

WEB CODE jcd-0213
PHSchool.com

Realidades ❶

Capítulo 2B

Nombre _____

Fecha _____

Hora _____

Practice Workbook **2B–7**

¡Aquí está!

It was a very busy afternoon in your classroom, and things got a little out of order. Write eight sentences describing where things are to help your teacher find everything.

| Modelo | _El escritorio está debajo de la computadora_____ . |

1. _____

2. _____

3. _____

4. _____

5. _____

6. _____

7. _____

8. _____

Go Online WEB CODE jcd-0215
PHSchool.com

Realidades 1

Capítulo 2B

Nombre _____

Hora _____

Fecha _____

Practice Workbook **2B–8**

Repaso

Across

2.

5. la ____ de clases

9.

12.

14.

15. La ____ está detrás del pupitre.
16. La computadora está en la ____.
17. *window*
19. *diskette*

20.

Down

1. *pencil sharpener*
3. no está encima de, está ____ de

4.

6.
7. al ____ de: *next to*
8. no delante

10.

11.
13. *mouse*
18. No estás aquí, estás ____.

Realidades 1

Capítulo 2B

Nombre _____

Fecha _____

Hora _____

Practice Workbook **2B–9**

Organizer

I. Vocabulary

Items in my classroom

_____

_____

_____

_____

_____

_____

_____

_____

_____

_____

_____

Words to tell the location of things

_____

_____

_____

_____

_____

_____

_____

_____

_____

II. Grammar

1. The forms of **estar** are: _____ _____

   _____ _____

   _____ _____

2. _____ and _____ are the singular definite articles in

   Spanish. Their plurals are _____ and _____ .

3. The singular indefinite articles are _____ and _____ in

   Spanish. Their plurals are _____ and _____ .

Go Online WEB CODE jcd-0216
PHSchool.com

Realidades ❶

Capítulo 3A

Nombre _____

Hora _____

Fecha _____

Practice Workbook **3A–1**

Tus comidas favoritas

You are getting ready to travel as an exchange student to Spain and you are e-mailing your host family your opinions on different foods. Circle the name of the food item that best completes each sentence below.

1. En el desayuno, yo como _____

   a. cereal.   **b.** un sándwich.

2. Mi comida favorita es _____

   a. el té.   **b.** la pizza.

3. Mi fruta favorita es _____

   a. la fresa.   **b.** la sopa.

4. Para beber, yo prefiero _____

   a. los huevos.   **b.** los refrescos.

5. A mí me gusta el jugo de _____

   a. manzana.   **b.** salchicha.

6. En el almuerzo, yo como _____

   a. un sándwich.   **b.** cereal.

7. Cuando hace frío, yo bebo _____

   a. té helado.   **b.** té.

8. Un BLT es un sándwich de verduras con _____

   a. jamón.   **b.** tocino.

9. Cuando voy a un partido de béisbol, yo como _____

   a. la sopa.   **b.** un perrito caliente.

10. En un sándwich, prefiero _____

    a. el queso.   **b.** el yogur.

¿Desayuno o almuerzo?

Your aunt owns a restaurant and is making her breakfast and lunch menus for the day. Help her by writing the foods and beverages that you think she should serve for each meal in the right places on the menus. Some words may be used more than once.

Go Online WEB CODE jcd-0301
PHSchool.com

Realidades 1

Capítulo 3A

Nombre _____

Hora _____

Fecha _____

Practice Workbook **3A–3**

Tus preferencias

You are asking Corazón, an exchange student from Venezuela, about various food items that she likes to eat. Use the pictures to help you complete Corazón's answers. Follow the model.

Modelo

TÚ: ¿Tú comes galletas?

CORAZÓN: No. _Yo como huevos_ .

1.

TÚ: ¿Tú comes salchichas?

CORAZÓN: No. _____ .

2.

TÚ: ¿Te gusta más _____ o _____?

CORAZÓN: _____ el café.

3.

TÚ: ¿Tú bebes mucha limonada?

CORAZÓN: No. _____ .

4.

TÚ: ¿Tú comes mucha sopa de verduras?

CORAZÓN: No. _____ .

5.

TÚ: ¿Tú bebes té helado?

CORAZÓN: No. _____ .

6.

TÚ: ¿Tú compartes el desayuno con amigos?

CORAZÓN: No. _____ .

Realidades 1

Capítulo 3A

Nombre _____

Fecha _____

Hora _____

Practice Workbook **3A–4**

¿Qué comes?

Carolina, the new exchange student, is having a hard time figuring out the kinds of foods that people like to eat. Answer her questions in complete sentences, using **¡Qué asco!** and **¡Por supuesto!** in at least one answer each.

1. ¿Comes hamburguesas con plátanos?

   _____

2. ¿Comes el sándwich de jamón y queso en el almuerzo?

   _____

3. ¿Bebes leche en el desayuno?

   _____

4. ¿Te gusta la pizza con la ensalada de frutas?

   _____

5. ¿Comes papas fritas en el desayuno?

   _____

6. ¿Compartes la comida con tu familia?

   _____

7. ¿Comes un perro caliente todos los días?

   _____

8. ¿Te encantan las galletas con leche?

   _____

Go Online WEB CODE jcd-0302
PHSchool.com

Realidades 1

Capítulo 3A

Nombre _____

Hora _____

Fecha _____

Practice Workbook **3A–5**

El verbo correcto

A. Fill in the chart below with all the forms of the verbs given.

	yo	tú	él/ella/Ud.	nosotros/ nosotras	vosotros/ vosotras	ellos/ ellas/Uds.
comer			come		coméis	
beber		bebes			bebéis	
comprender	comprendo				comprendéis	
escribir				escribimos	escribís	
compartir					compartís	comparten

B. Now, using the verbs from Part A, write the missing verb to complete each sentence below.

1. Antonio _____ sus papas fritas con Amelia.

2. Uds. _____ los sándwiches de queso.

3. Yo _____ las salchichas en el desayuno.

4. Nosotros _____ el té helado.

5. Ana _____ la tarea.

6. Tú _____ una carta al profesor.

7. Yo _____ el pan con Jorge.

8. Él _____ jugo de naranja en el desayuno.

9. Nosotros _____ con un lápiz.

10. Paula y Guillermo hablan y _____ español.

11. ¿_____ tú leche en el desayuno?

12. Manolo y Federico _____ las galletas con Susana.

Realidades 1

Capítulo 3A

Nombre _____

Fecha _____

Hora _____

Practice Workbook **3A–6**

¿Qué te gusta?

A. List your food preferences in the blanks below.

Me gusta	Me gustan	Me encanta	Me encantan
			los sándwiches
_____	_____	_____	_____
_____	_____	_____	_____
			_____

B. Now, organize your preferences into complete sentences. Follow the model.

Modelo   *Me encantan los sándwiches.* _____

1. _____
2. _____
3. _____
4. _____
5. _____
6. _____
7. _____
8. _____

C. Using the words given, write a sentence about each food. Follow the model.

Modelo   El té (encantar) *Me encanta el té.* _____

1. los plátanos (gustar) _____
2. la pizza (encantar) _____
3. las papas fritas (encantar) _____
4. el pan (gustar) _____

Go Online WEB CODE jcd-0304
PHSchool.com

Realidades ①

Capítulo 3A

Nombre _____

Fecha _____

Hora _____

Practice Workbook **3A–7**

Mini-conversaciones

Fill in the blanks in the mini-conversations below with the most logical question or answer.

1. —¿Comparten Uds. el sándwich de jamón y queso?

   —Sí, nosotros _____ el sándwich.

2. —¿_____ tú todos los días?

   —No, nunca corro. No me gusta.

3. —¿_____ en el desayuno?

   —¡Qué asco! No me gustan los plátanos.

4. —¿_____?

   —Sí, profesora. Comprendemos la lección.

5. —¿_____?

   —Mi jugo favorito es el jugo de manzana.

6. —¿_____?

   —Más o menos. Me gusta más la pizza.

7. —¿_____?

   —¡Por supuesto! Me encanta el cereal.

Realidades ❶

Capítulo 3A

Nombre _____

Hora _____

Fecha _____

Practice Workbook **3A–8**

Repaso

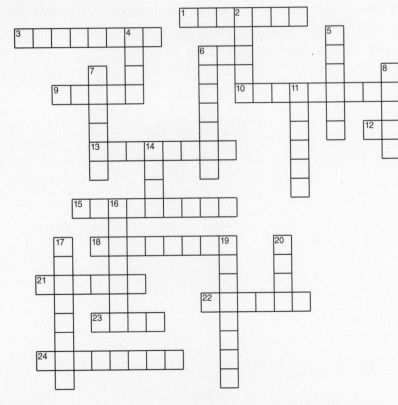

© Pearson Education, Inc. All rights reserved.

Down

2. más o ___
4. ¡Qué ___! No me gustan los guisantes.

5.

6.
7. el té ___
8. las ___ fritas
11. *food*

14.

16.  un jugo de ___

17. No como carne. Me gusta la sopa de ___.
19. En los Estados Unidos el ___ es un sándwich y algo de beber.
20. un ___ de naranja

Across

1. *always*
3. El Monstruo Comegalletas come muchas ___.
6. el ___ tostado
9. Me gusta el sándwich de jamón y ___.

10.

12.

13. Muchas personas comen cereales con leche en el ___

15. ¿Te gusta ___ el almuerzo con tus amigos?
18. Me gusta la ___ de frutas, no de lechuga.
21. un yogur de ___

22.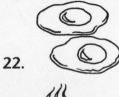

23.

24. el perrito ___

Organizer

I. Vocabulary

Breakfast foods

_____

_____

_____

_____

Lunch foods

_____

_____

_____

_____

Beverages

_____

_____

_____

Words to express likes/dislikes

_____

_____

_____

II. Grammar

1. The **-er** verb endings are: -_____   -_____

      -_____   -_____

      -_____   -_____

   Now conjugate the verb **beber**:   _____   _____

      _____   _____

      _____   _____

2. The **-ir** verb endings are: -_____   -_____

      -_____   -_____

      -_____   -_____

   Now conjugate the verb **compartir**:   _____   _____

      _____   _____

      _____   _____

3. To use **me gusta** and **me encanta** to talk about plural nouns, you add the letter _____ to the end of the verb.

WEB CODE jcd-0306
PHSchool.com

Repaso del capítulo ━ *Vocabulario y gramática* **57**

Realidades 1

Capítulo 3B

Nombre _____

Hora _____

Fecha _____

Practice Workbook **3B–1**

¡A cenar!

A. You are having a party, and you need to make a shopping list. Write at least three items that you might want to buy under each category. You may use vocabulary from other chapters.

La ensalada de frutas:

_____

_____

_____

_____

Las verduras:

_____

_____

_____

_____

La carne:

_____

_____

_____

_____

Bebemos:

_____

_____

_____

_____

B. Now write three things your guests might like to eat after dinner.

_____

_____

_____

Más comida

A. Name the most logical food category to which each group of items belongs.

1. el bistec, el pollo, el pescado _____

2. las zanahorias, la cebolla, los guisantes _____

3. las uvas, las manzanas _____

4. el postre, la mantequilla _____

B. Now, answer the following questions logically in complete sentences.

1. ¿Debemos comer las uvas, el helado o los pasteles para mantener la salud?

_____

2. ¿Es sabrosa la ensalada de frutas con las papas o con los plátanos?

_____

3. ¿Comemos la mantequilla con el pan tostado o con el bistec?

_____

4. ¿Bebemos los refrescos o el agua para mantener la salud?

_____

C. Using the foods below, write sentences telling whether we should or shouldn't eat or drink each thing to maintain good health. Follow the model.

Modelo   el agua *Debemos beber el agua para mantener la salud.* ____

1. los tomates _____

2. las grasas _____

3. los plátanos _____

4. las uvas _____

5. la mantequilla _____

6. la leche _____

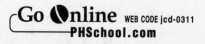

Realidades **1**

Nombre _____

Hora _____

Capítulo 3B

Fecha _____

Practice Workbook **3B–3**

La respuesta perfecta

You are learning about fitness and nutrition at school, and your friends want to know more. Answer their questions or respond to their statements in complete sentences.

1. ¿Es el tomate bueno para la salud?

_____

2. ¿Por qué caminas todos los días?

_____

3. ¿La mantequilla es buena para la salud?

_____

4. Creo que las grasas son horribles.

_____

5. ¿Qué debes hacer para mantener la salud?

_____

6. ¿Prefieres levantar pesas o caminar?

_____

7. Creo que los espaguetis son sabrosos. ¿Y tú?

_____

Go Online WEB CODE jcd-0312
PHSchool.com

¿Qué comes?

Angel is asking his friend Estela about foods she likes. Fill in the blanks with the foods suggested by the pictures, then complete Estela's answers.

1. —¿Te gustan _____?

   —No, _____.

2. —¿Prefieres _____ con _____
   en el almuerzo o en la cena?

   —_____ en el almuerzo.

3. —¿Te gustan _____?

   —Sí, _____.

4. —¿Prefieres _____ de chocolate o de fruta?

   —_____ de chocolate.

5. —¿Comes _____?

   —Sí, _____.

6. —¿Siempre comes _____ en el almuerzo?

   —No, _____.

7. —¿Te gusta el _____ con _____?

   —Sí, _____.

Realidades 1

Capítulo 3B

Nombre _____

Fecha _____

Hora _____

Practice Workbook **3B–5**

Las descripciones

A. Fill in the chart below with the singular and plural, masculine and feminine forms of the adjectives given.

Masculine		Feminine	
singular	plural	singular	plural
sabroso			
	prácticos		
		fácil	
	aburridos		
			difíciles
divertido			
		artística	
			buenas
trabajador			

B. Now, complete the sentences below, using some of the words from the chart above. There may be more than one right answer.

1. La ensalada de frutas es _____ para la salud.

2. Me gustan mis clases; son _____.

3. La tarea de matemáticas es _____.

4. Te gustan las computadoras porque son _____.

5. Mi profesor no come pescado porque cree que no es _____.

6. Mis amigos son _____; dibujan muy bien.

7. Tus amigos son muy _____; trabajan mucho.

8. Esquiar y nadar son actividades muy _____.

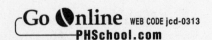

WEB CODE jcd-0313
PHSchool.com

¿Cómo son?

Describe the following people using the pictures as clues. Use a form of **ser** plus an adjective. Follow the model.

Modelo

¿Cómo _____ *es* _____ él?

Él es popular _____.

1.

¿Cómo _____ él?

_____.

2.

¿Cómo _____ ella?

_____.

3.

¿Cómo _____ ellas?

_____.

4.

¿Cómo _____ ellos?

_____.

5.

¿Cómo _____ nosotras?

_____.

6.

¿Cómo _____ yo?

_____.

Realidades 1

Capítulo 3B

Nombre _____

Fecha _____

Hora _____

Practice Workbook **3B–7**

La buena salud

Your cousin Eva has started a new diet and exercise program, and she has sent you an e-mail telling you all about it. Read her e-mail and answer the questions below in complete sentences.

> Hola,
>
> Para mantener la salud, como muchas verduras y frutas cada día. ¡Creo que son sabrosas! Yo hago ejercicio también. Me gusta caminar, pero prefiero levantar pesas. Siempre bebo mucha agua, y es mi bebida favorita. No debemos comer los pasteles, porque son malos para la salud. ¿Estás de acuerdo?

1. ¿Qué come Eva para mantener la salud?

   _____

2. ¿Eva hace ejercicio?

   _____

3. ¿A Eva le gustan las frutas?

   _____

4. ¿Qué prefiere hacer Eva para mantener la salud?

   _____

5. ¿Cuál es la bebida favorita de Eva?

   _____

6. ¿Por qué no debemos comer los pasteles?

   _____

Realidades ❶

Capítulo 3B

Nombre _____

Hora _____

Fecha _____

Practice Workbook **3B–8**

Repaso

Across

3. el ___

5.

6. Prefiero las ensaladas de ___ y tomate.

8. el ___

10. Debes comer bien para mantener la ___.

12. *drinks*

13. el ___

16. *something*

18. Tengo ___. Necesito comer.

20. estoy de ___

22. Los ___ no son buenos para la salud pero son sabrosos.

24. ___ comer bien para mantener la salud.

Down

1. *meat*

2. un ___

4. las ___ verdes

7. los ___

9. Yo prefiero ___ la salud y comer bien.

11. las ___

14. *carrots*

15. Me gusta la comida de tu mamá. Es muy ___ .

17.

19.

21. *dinner*

23. ___ los días; siempre

Organizer

I. Vocabulary

Fruits and vegetables

_____

_____

_____

_____

Starches

_____

_____

_____

_____

General food terms

_____

_____

_____

_____

Types of exercise

_____

_____

_____

_____

II. Grammar

1. Adjectives are _____ when describing one person or thing, and _____ when describing more than one person or thing.

2. To make an adjective plural, add _____ if the last letter is a vowel and _____ if the last letter is a consonant.

3. The forms of **ser** are: _____ _____

    _____ _____

    _____ _____

Go Online WEB CODE jcd-0316
PHSchool.com

¿Qué hacen?

What do the people in your neighborhood like to do in their free time? Complete the following sentences based on the pictures.

1.

La Sra. García lee un libro en

_____.

2.

Jesús levanta pesas en

_____.

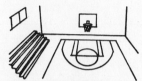

3.

Los lunes tengo _____

con el Sr. Casals.

4.

A Pedro le gusta pasar tiempo en _____

cuando tiene tiempo libre.

5.

Elena y Tomás prefieren ir al _____

los viernes.

6.

A mí me gusta ir a _____

cuando hace calor.

7.

A Sara le gusta caminar en

_____.

8.

Me gusta ir al _____

para comer.

Realidades ❶

Capítulo 4A

Nombre _____

Hora _____

Fecha _____

Practice Workbook **4A–2**

¿Adónde vas?

Where do you go to do the following things? Write your answers in complete sentences. Follow the model.

Modelo esquiar   _Voy a las montañas para esquiar._

1. trabajar   _____

2. leer, estudiar   _____

3. hablar español   _____

4. correr, caminar   _____

5. ir de compras   _____

6. tocar el piano   _____

7. comer, beber   _____

8. ver una película   _____

9. nadar   _____

10. hacer ejercicio   _____

11. estar con amigos   _____

12. levantar pesas   _____

Go Online WEB CODE jcd-0401
PHSchool.com

Realidades ❶

Capítulo 4A

Nombre _____

Hora _____

Fecha _____

Practice Workbook **4A–3**

¿Qué hacen?

An exchange student from Chile wants to know where people go to do certain activities. Complete each conversation with the verb suggested by the first picture, then answer the questions based on the second illustration.

Modelo

—Cuando _____ves_____ una película, ¿adónde vas?

—_____Voy al cine_____.

1.

—Cuando _____, ¿adónde vas?

—_____.

2.

—Cuando _____, ¿adónde vas?

—_____.

3.

—Cuando _____, ¿adónde vas?

—_____.

4.

—Cuando _____, ¿adónde vas?

—_____.

5.

—Cuando _____, ¿adónde vas?

—_____.

6.

—Cuando _____, ¿adónde vas?

—_____.

Realidades 1

Capítulo 4A

Nombre _____

Fecha _____

Hora _____

Practice Workbook **4A–4**

El horario de Tito

Look at Tito's schedule for part of the month of February. Then answer the questions about his activities in complete sentences.

FEBRERO						
lunes	martes	miércoles	jueves	viernes	sábado	domingo
8 trabajar	9 nadar	10 estudiar en la biblioteca	11 trabajar	12 ir al cine	13 ir al gimnasio	14 ir a la iglesia
15 trabajar	16 practicar karate	17 estudiar en la biblioteca	18 trabajar	19 ir al cine	20 ir al gimnasio	21 ir a la iglesia
22 trabajar	23 levantar pesas	24 estudiar en la biblioteca	25 trabajar	26 ir al cine	27 ir al gimnasio	28 ir a la iglesia

1. ¿Qué hace Tito los viernes?

_____

2. ¿Cuándo estudia Tito en la biblioteca?

_____

3. ¿Cuándo hace ejercicio Tito?

_____

4. Generalmente, ¿cuándo trabaja Tito?

_____

5. ¿Qué hace Tito los lunes?

_____

6. ¿Cuándo va a la iglesia Tito?

_____

7. ¿Qué hace Tito los fines de semana?

_____

Go Online WEB CODE jcd-0402 PHSchool.com

Realidades ❶

Capítulo 4A

Nombre _____

Hora _____

Fecha _____

Practice Workbook **4A–5**

Las actividades favoritas

Students are making plans for what they will do after school. Complete their conversations with the correct forms of the verb **ir**.

1. LOLIS: Hoy, (yo) _____ al parque después de las clases.

ELIA: ¡Qué bien! María y yo _____ al cine.

LOLIS: Mi amigo Pablo también _____ al cine hoy.

2. MARTA: Hola, Juan. ¿Adónde _____ ?

JUAN: Pues, _____ a la clase de inglés, pero después

_____ al centro comercial. ¿Y tú?

MARTA: Pues, mis padres _____ a la playa y yo

_____ con ellos.

JUAN: ¡Qué bueno! ¿Cuándo _____ Uds.?

MARTA: Nosotros _____ después de las clases.

3. RODOLFO: ¡Hola, Pablo, Felipe!

PABLO Y FELIPE: ¡Hola, Rodolfo!

RODOLFO: ¿Adónde _____ Uds.?

PABLO: Pues, yo _____ a casa con unos amigos.

FELIPE: Yo no _____ con él. _____ a la mezquita.

¿Y tú?

RODOLFO: Catrina y yo _____ a la piscina. Ella _____

al gimnasio más tarde.

PABLO: Mi amiga Elena _____ al gimnasio con ella. Creo que

ellas _____ a las cinco.

FELIPE: Es muy tarde. Tengo que _____ . ¡Hasta luego!

La pregunta perfecta

A. Complete the following questions with the correct question words.

1. ¿_____ es el chico más alto de la clase?

2. ¿_____ vas al cine? ¿Hoy?

3. ¿_____ es tu número de teléfono?

4. ¿_____ te llamas?

5. ¿_____ vas después de las clases hoy?

6. ¿_____ está mi libro de español?

7. ¿_____ es esto?

8. ¿_____ años tienes?

B. Now, form your own questions using some of the question words above.

1. ¿_____?

2. ¿_____?

3. ¿_____?

4. ¿_____?

5. ¿_____?

6. ¿_____?

7. ¿_____?

Go Online WEB CODE jcd-0404
PHSchool.com

Realidades ❶

Capítulo 4A

Nombre _____

Hora _____

Fecha _____

Practice Workbook **4A–7**

¿Qué haces?

You are talking with your parents about your plans for the evening. They have lots of questions. Your answers are given below. Write your parents' questions in the spaces provided.

TUS PADRES: ¿_____?

TÚ: Voy a un restaurante.

TUS PADRES: ¿_____?

TÚ: Voy con unos amigos.

TUS PADRES: ¿_____?

TÚ: Ellos se llaman Roberto y Ana.

TUS PADRES: ¿_____?

TÚ: Roberto y Ana son de México.

TUS PADRES: ¿_____?

TÚ: Pues, Roberto es inteligente, trabajador y paciente.

TUS PADRES: ¿_____?

TÚ: Ana es deportista y estudiosa.

TUS PADRES: ¿_____?

TÚ: Después, nosotros vamos al cine.

TUS PADRES: ¿_____?

TÚ: ¿Después? Pues, voy a casa. ¡Uds. hacen muchas preguntas!

Realidades ❶

Capítulo 4A

Nombre _____

Fecha _____

Hora _____

Practice Workbook **4A–8**

Repaso

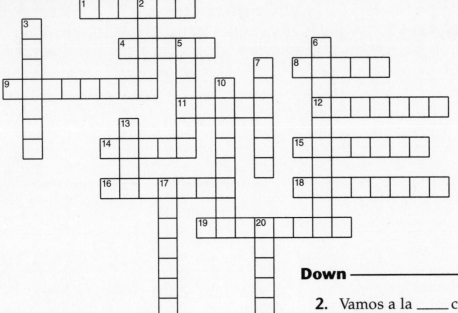

Across

1. *temple*

4.

8. ¡No me _____!

9. *mosque*

11. –¿Con _____ vas al cine?
    – Con Ana.

12. Tengo que ir a la _____ de piano.

14. No tengo tiempo _____.

15. Para la Navidad todos van de _____.

16. *after*

18. Me gusta la _____ *Desperado*.

19.

Down

2. Vamos a la _____ cuando hace calor.

3.

5. Me gusta caminar en el _____.

6.

7. el _____ comercial

10. Voy al _____ para levantar pesas.

13. Vamos al _____ para ver una película.

17.

20. Vas al _____ para trabajar.

Organizer

I. Vocabulary

Some of my favorite places

_____

_____

_____

_____

_____

_____

Words to talk about other places

_____

_____

_____

_____

_____

_____

Interrogative words

_____

_____

_____

_____

_____

_____

Phrases related to leisure activities

_____

_____

_____

_____

II. Grammar

1. The forms of the verb **ir** are: _____ _____

   _____ _____

   _____ _____

2. **A.** In order to get information in English, we use the words *who, what, where, when, why,* and *how*. In Spanish these words are: _____, _____,

   _____, _____, _____ y _____ .

   B. When asking a question in Spanish, the verb comes _____ the subject.

¿Eres deportista?

Write the name of the sport or activity indicated by the art.

1. _____

2. _____

3. _____

4. _____

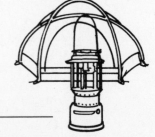

5. _____

6. _____

7. _____

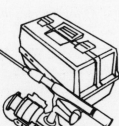

8. _____

9. _____

Go Online WEB CODE jcd-0411
PHSchool.com

Las invitaciones

You and your friends are making plans for the weekend. Complete your friends' invitations with the activities suggested by the pictures. Then accept the offers using complete sentences. Follow the model.

Modelo

—¿Te gustaría _____*ir al cine*_____ este fin de semana?

—_____*Sí, me gustaría ir al cine*_____.

1.

—¿Puedes _____ este fin de semana?

—_____.

2.

—¿Quieres _____ este fin de semana?

—_____.

3.

—¿Puedes _____ este fin de semana?

—_____.

4.

—¿Te gustaría _____ este fin de semana?

—_____.

5.

—¿Quieres _____ este fin de semana?

—_____.

Realidades ①

Capítulo 4B

Nombre _____

Hora _____

Fecha _____

Practice Workbook **4B–3**

¿Cómo están?

You have just arrived at school and are asking how your friends are doing. Using the pictures to help you, fill in the blanks with the correct form of **estar** and the appropriate adjective. Don't forget to make the adjective agree with the subject!

1. —¿Cómo está ella?

—_____.

2. —¿Cómo está él?

—_____.

3. —¿Cómo están ellos?

—_____.

4. —¿Cómo están ellas?

—_____.

5. —¿Cómo están los estudiantes?

—_____.

6. —¿Cómo está él?

—_____.

Go Online WEB CODE jcd-0412
PHSchool.com

Realidades ①

Capítulo 4B

Nombre _____

Hora _____

Fecha _____

Practice Workbook **4B–4**

¿A qué hora?

Lucía is very busy on the weekends. Answer the questions about her schedule using complete sentences.

Modelo ¿A qué hora usa la computadora?

Usa la computadora a las siete y media de la noche.

1. ¿A qué hora tiene que trabajar Lucía?

_____

2. ¿A qué hora va a casa?

_____

3. ¿Qué hacen Lucía y su amiga a las ocho de la mañana?

_____

4. ¿A qué hora come la cena Lucía?

_____

5. ¿Cuándo estudian ella y su amigo?

_____

6. ¿Adónde va Lucía esta noche? ¿A qué hora?

_____

Realidades 1

Capítulo 4B

Nombre _____

Hora _____

Fecha _____

Practice Workbook **4B–5**

Los planes

It is 10:00 Saturday morning, and you and your friends are making plans for the afternoon and evening. Using a form of **ir** + **a** + *infinitive,* write complete sentences about everyone's plans. Follow the model.

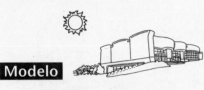 María

Modelo _____María va a ir de compras esta tarde_____.

 Ana y yo

1. _____.

 Pablo

2. _____.

 Yo

3. _____.

 Mis amigos

4. _____.

 Tú

5. _____.

 Nosotros

6. _____.

 Ud.

7. _____.

 Ana y Lorena

8. _____.

Go Online WEB CODE jcd-0413
PHSchool.com

Realidades ①

Capítulo 4B

Nombre _____

Fecha _____

Hora _____

Practice Workbook **4B-6**

Demasiadas preguntas

Your friends are asking you to make plans for this weekend, but you are not able to do anything that they have suggested. Using the pictures to help you, respond to their questions using **ir** + **a** + *infinitive*. Follow the model.

Modelo

¿Puedes ir al partido mañana?

No, no puedo. Voy a correr mañana _____.

¿Quieres ir al partido esta noche?

1. _____.

¿Te gustaría ir al cine conmigo esta noche?

2. _____.

¿Quieres jugar al golf esta tarde?

3. _____.

¿Puedes jugar videojuegos conmigo el viernes?

4. _____.

¿Te gustaría ir de compras mañana por la noche?

5. _____.

¿Te gustaría ir al baile conmigo esta noche?

6. _____.

¿Quieres ir a la biblioteca conmigo?

7. _____.

¿Puedes ir de cámping conmigo este fin de semana?

8. _____.

¿A qué juegas?

Friends are talking about the sports that they enjoy playing. Write the correct form of the verb **jugar** to complete each sentence.

1. —¿Marta juega al vóleibol?

   —Sí, Rodrigo y ella _____ todos los días.

2. —Oye, ¿puedes jugar al básquetbol con nosotros?

   —Lo siento, pero no _____ bien.

3. —¿A qué juegan Uds.?

   —Nosotros _____ al golf.

4. —Ellas juegan al tenis muy bien, ¿no?

   —Sí, _____ muy bien.

5. —¿_____ Ud. al básquetbol a la una?

   —No. Tengo que ir a un concierto.

6. —Yo juego al fútbol hoy.

   —¡Ay, me encanta el fútbol! ¡_____ contigo!

7. —¿Tú y Manuel jugáis al béisbol esta tarde?

   —Sí. ¡_____ todos los días!

8. —¿Qué hace Luz esta noche?

   —Ella _____ al vóleibol a las ocho.

Go Online WEB CODE jcd-0414
PHSchool.com

Realidades

Capítulo 4B

Nombre _____

Fecha _____

Hora _____

Practice Workbook **4B–8**

Repaso

Across

3. No puedo jugar. Estoy ____ ocupado.

4. *sad*

5.

7. Me gusta ver el ____ de béisbol.

9. yo sé, tú ____

10. Lo ____, pero no puedo.

12.  el fútbol ____

15.

17. El *Jitterbug* es un ____.

19. *Great!*

20. Vamos al ____ para escuchar música.

21. *with me*

Down

1. Vamos a la ____ de cumpleaños de Paco.

2.

6. *afternoon*; la ____

7. me gusta ir de *fishing*

8. el ____ de semana

11. Ella trabaja mucho, siempre está ____.

13.

14. Es después de la tarde; la ____.

16. *Hey!*

17.

18. Voy a la escuela a las siete de la ____.

Repaso del capítulo ━ *Crucigrama* **83**

Organizer

I. Vocabulary

Words to talk about activities

_____

_____

_____

Words to describe how you feel

_____

_____

_____

Words to accept or decline an invitation

_____

_____

_____

_____

Names of sports

_____

_____

_____

_____

Words to say when something happens

_____

_____

_____

_____

II. Grammar

1. The forms of the verb **jugar** are: _____ _____

   _____ _____

   _____ _____

2. The preposition **con** becomes _____ to mean "with me" and _____ to mean "with you."

3. To say you are going to do something, you use the verb _____ + _____ + the action you are going to perform.

Go Online WEB CODE jcd-0416
PHSchool.com

La familia

A. Patricia is telling you about her family. Label each person in her family tree with a word that describes his or her relationship to Patricia. You may use some words more than once.

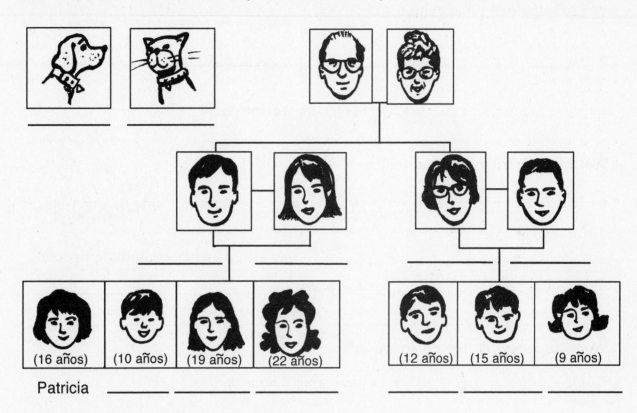

(16 años) (10 años) (19 años) (22 años)   (12 años) (15 años) (9 años)

Patricia _____ _____ _____   _____ _____ _____

B. Now, answer the following questions by circling **sí** or **no**.

1. ¿Patricia tiene hermanastros?   Sí   No

2. ¿Patricia tiene hermanas mayores?   Sí   No

3. ¿Patricia tiene dieciséis años?   Sí   No

4. ¿Patricia tiene tres primos menores?   Sí   No

5. ¿Patricia tiene dos abuelas?   Sí   No

¿Quién es?

A. Complete the sentences below with the correct family relationships.

1. Mi ___ ___ (◯) es la esposa de mi tío.

2. Mis ___ ___ ___ (◯) ___ ___ ___ ___ son los hijos de mis padres.

3. Mi ___ ___ (◯) ___ ___ es el hijo del hermano de mi padre.

4. Mi (◯) ___ ___ ___ ___ ___ es la madre de mi madre.

5. Mi ___ ___ ___ ___ ___ ___ ___ (◯) ___ es el esposo de mi madre (no es mi padre).

6. Yo soy la ___ ___ ___ (◯) de mis padres.

7. Mi ___ ___ (◯) ___ es la hija de la hermana de mi padre.

8. Mis (◯) ___ ___ ___ son los hermanos de mis padres.

9. Mamá y papá son mis ___ ___ (◯) ___ ___ ___ .

10. Mis ___ (◯) ___ ___ ___ ___ (◯) ___ ___ ___ ___ son las hijas de la esposa de mi padre (no son mis hermanas).

B. Now, unscramble the circled letters to come up with another member of the family.

___ ___ ___ ___ ___ ___ ___ ___ ___ ___ ___ ___

Go Online WEB CODE jcd-0501
PHSchool.com

¡Una fiesta inesperada (*a surprise party*)!

The Rodríguez family is giving their older son Tomás a surprise birthday party. Complete their conversation, using the most logical word from the word bank.

luces	la piñata	tiene	decoraciones
dulces	pastel	celebrar	sólo
globos	sacar fotos	regalos	

MAMÁ: Vamos a hacer el plan porque vamos a _____ el cumpleaños

de Tomás. Él _____ doce años.

TÍA LULÚ: Sí, ¡vamos a celebrar! Primero, necesitamos un _____ para

comer ¿no? ¡Qué sabroso!

MAMÁ: Sí. Y necesitamos unas _____ perfectas. Vamos a necesitar un

globo y una luz.

TÍA LULÚ: ¿_____ *un* globo y *una* luz? ¡No, necesitamos muchos

_____ y muchas _____! También

necesitamos papel picado.

PABLITO: Oye, ¡yo tengo una cámara fabulosa! Puedo _____ en la

fiesta cuando Tomás abre los _____.

MAMÁ: Sí, Pablito. ¡Muchas gracias! Y finalmente, pueden romper

_____. ¿Tenemos _____?

TÍA LULÚ: Sí, tenemos muchos dulces.

PABLITO: ¡Qué buena fiesta!

La celebración

Raúl is explaining how he and his family are preparing for his sister's birthday party. Read his description and answer the questions that follow in complete sentences.

> Hoy es el cumpleaños de mi hermana menor, Gabriela. Mis padres y yo preparamos la fiesta. Mi mamá decora con el papel picado y las luces. Mi papá tiene los regalos y los globos. Yo preparo la mesa con los globos y el pastel. También tengo la cámara porque voy a hacer un video de la fiesta.
>
> Sólo nuestra familia va a estar aquí, pero con todos mis primos, mis tíos y mis abuelos tenemos muchas personas. A las cinco mi hermana va a estar aquí y la fiesta va a empezar.

1. ¿Quién es Gabriela? _____

2. ¿Para quién es la fiesta? _____

3. ¿Qué clase de fiesta es? _____

4. ¿Con qué decora Raúl? _____

5. ¿Qué tiene el papá? _____

6. ¿Qué va a hacer Raúl? _____

7. ¿Quiénes van a estar en la fiesta? _____

_____

8. ¿A qué hora va a empezar la fiesta? _____

Go Online WEB CODE jcd-0502
PHSchool.com

Conversaciones

You overhear a group of students talking. Fill in the blanks in their conversations with the correct forms of the verb **tener**.

1. FRANCO: Hola, Carmen. ¿Qué tienes en la mano?

   CARMEN: (Yo) _____ un regalo para mi primo. Es su cumpleaños.

   FRANCO: Ah, ¿sí? ¿Cuántos años _____?

   CARMEN: _____ doce años.

   FRANCO: Mis primos también _____ doce años.

2. ELENA: ¡Oye, Carlos! ¿Cuántos años _____?

   CARLOS: ¿Yo? Yo _____ quince años. ¿Por qué?

   ELENA: Porque mi hermano y yo _____ una prima de quince

   años que _____ que ir a un baile el viernes. ¿(Tú)

   _____ planes?

   CARLOS: ¿El viernes? No, no _____ otros planes.

3. PABLO: Hola, José. Hola, Manolo. ¿(Uds.) _____ un dólar?

   JOSÉ: Sí, yo _____ un dólar.   ¿Por qué?

   PABLO: Porque yo _____ hambre y quiero comprar un perrito

   caliente.

   MANOLO: ¿La cafetería _____ perritos calientes buenos?

   PABLO: Sí. ¿Quieres uno?

   JOSÉ: Sí, pero primero Manolo y yo _____ que ir a clase.

   PABLO: También _____ que ir a clase.

Realidades ❶

Capítulo 5A

Nombre _____

Hora _____

Fecha _____

Practice Workbook **5A–6**

¿De quién es?

A. Fill in the following chart with the masculine and feminine, singular and plural forms of the possessive adjectives indicated.

hijo	tía	abuelos	hermanas
			mis hermanas
	tu tía		
su hijo			
		nuestros abuelos	
vuestro hijo	*vuestra tía*	*vuestros abuelos*	*vuestras hermanas*

B. Now, complete the following sentences by writing in the possessive adjective that corresponds with the English adjective in parentheses. Follow the model.

Modelo (*my*) _____Mi_____ abuela es vieja.

1. (*our*) _____ abuelos van a la casa para hablar con nosotros.

2. (*your*) Sara, gracias por _____ libro.

3. (*my*) _____ prima es de Tejas.

4. (*your*) ¿Tienen mucha tarea en _____ clase de matemáticas?

5. (*their*) _____ tíos están en la oficina ahora.

6. (*my*) El perro come _____ galletas.

7. (*our*) Nosotros vamos a la escuela en _____ bicicletas.

8. (*your*) Profesor, ¿dónde está _____ oficina?

9. (*their*) _____ hijo es muy trabajador.

10. (*his*) _____ hermana está enferma.

Realidades 1

Capítulo 5A

Nombre _____

Hora _____

Fecha _____

Practice Workbook **5A–7**

Los regalos perfectos

Using the subjects below and the activities suggested by the pictures, write complete sentences about what your friends and relatives have for the party. Make sure you use the correct possessive adjective. Follow the model.

Mi primo Juan

Modelo *Mi primo Juan tiene su cámara.*

Mis tíos

1. _____

Alicia

2. _____

Tú

3. _____

Nosotros

4. _____

Yo

5. _____

Ud.

6. _____

La profesora Méndez

7. _____

Nosotras

8. _____

Realidades ❶

Capítulo 5A

Nombre _____

Hora _____

Fecha _____

Practice Workbook **5A–8**

Repaso

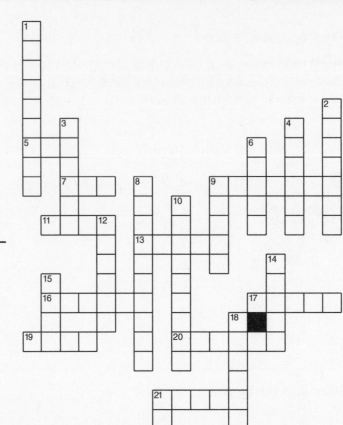

Across

5. La madre de mi primo es mi ____.

7. El hermano de mi padre es mi ____.

9. *sister*

11. ....☀️....

13. mi papá; el ____

16. La mamá de mi padre es mi ____.

17. Mi hermano y yo somos los ____ de nuestros padres.

19.

20.

21. mi mamá; la ____

Down

1. El esposo de mi madre; no es mi papá, es mi ____.

2. *brother*

3.

4. el papel ____

6.

8. ¡Feliz ____! ¿Cuántos años tienes?

9. Quiero ____ un video.

10. la madre de mi hermanastro; mi ____

12. Los hijos ____ la piñata.

14. Es el hermano de mi prima; mi ____.

15. ¿Quién ____ las fotos de la fiesta?

18. *parents*

21. no menor

Organizer

I. Vocabulary

To describe family relationships

_____

_____

_____

_____

_____

_____

_____

Items at a party

_____

_____

_____

_____

_____

Words to express possession

_____

_____

_____

_____

Activities at a party

_____

_____

_____

_____

II. Grammar

1. The forms of **tener** are: _____ _____

_____ _____

_____ _____

2. Possessive adjectives in Spanish are written as follows:

	Singular/Plural		Singular/Plural
my	_____ / _____	our	_____ / _____
your (familiar)	_____ / _____	your (pl., familiar)	_____ / _____
your (formal), his, hers	_____ / _____	your (pl., formal), their	_____ / _____

 WEB CODE jcd-0508
PHSchool.com

Repaso del capítulo ━ *Vocabulario y gramática* **93**

Realidades **1**

Capítulo 5B

Nombre _____

Hora _____

Fecha _____

Practice Workbook **5B–1**

Restaurante elegante

Label the following items with the correct word. Don't forget to use the correct definite article (**el** or **la**).

1. _____

2. _____

3. _____

4. _____

5. _____

6. _____

7. _____

8. _____

9. _____

10. _____

11. _____

Go Online WEB CODE jcd-0511
PHSchool.com

Las descripciones

You are telling your friends about some of your family members. Write descriptions of them in complete sentences. Follow the model.

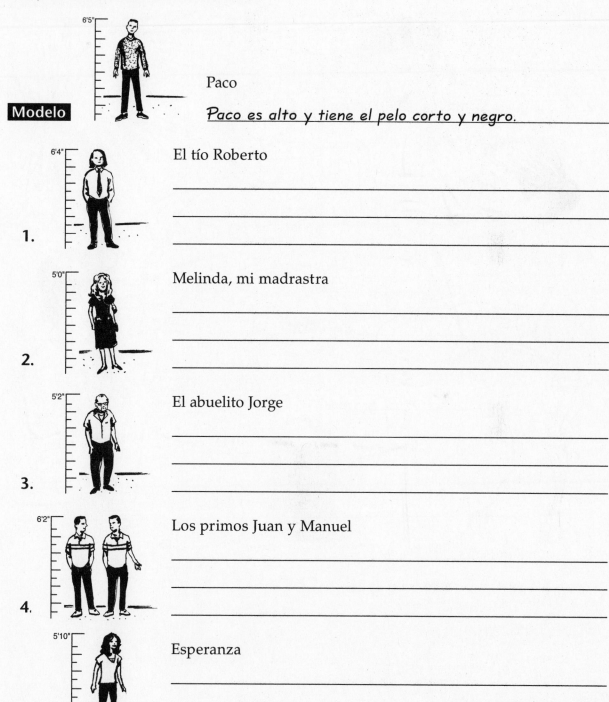

Paco

Modelo

Paco es alto y tiene el pelo corto y negro.

El tío Roberto

1. _____
_____
_____

Melinda, mi madrastra

2. _____
_____
_____

El abuelito Jorge

3. _____
_____
_____

Los primos Juan y Manuel

4. _____
_____
_____

Esperanza

5. _____
_____
_____

Realidades 1

Capítulo 5B

Nombre _____

Fecha _____

Hora _____

Practice Workbook **5B–3**

La palabra correcta

Complete the following mini-conversations with the most logical words or phrases from your vocabulary.

1. —¿Necesita Ud. algo?

—Sí, me _____ un tenedor.

2. —¿Te gusta la comida del Sr. Vargas?

—Sí, es deliciosa. ¡Qué _____!

3. —¿Quieres otra _____ de café?

—No, gracias.

4. —¿Desea Ud. un té helado?

—Sí, porque tengo _____.

5. —¿Qué vas a _____ de postre?

—Yo quiero el flan.

6. —¿Necesitan _____ más?

—Sí, la cuenta por favor.

7. —Muchas gracias.

—De _____.

8. —¿Qué quisiera Ud. de _____ _____?

—Me gustaría el arroz con pollo.

9. —¿Estás cansado?

—Sí, tengo _____.

10. —¿Bebes el café?

—Sí, porque tengo _____.

Go Online WEB CODE jcd-0512
PHSchool.com

Realidades 1

Capítulo 5B

Nombre _____

Fecha _____

Hora _____

Practice Workbook **5B–4**

Cita (*date*) en español

A. David and Rocío are on a date at a Spanish restaurant. Using the vocabulary you have learned in this chapter, write their possible responses to the waiter's questions. Use complete sentences.

CAMARERO: ¿Qué desean Uds. de plato principal?

DAVID: _____

ROCÍO: _____

CAMARERO: ¿Cómo está la comida?

DAVID: _____

ROCÍO: _____

CAMARERO: ¿Desean algo más?

DAVID: _____

ROCÍO: _____

B. Now, based on the waiter's responses, write what you think David or Rocío may have asked the waiter.

DAVID: ¿_____?

CAMARERO: Sí, le traigo una servilleta.

ROCÍO: ¿_____?

CAMARERO: Sí, ahora puede pedir algo de postre.

DAVID: ¿_____?

CAMARERO: Un café, por supuesto. ¿Tiene sueño?

WEB CODE jcd-0512
PHSchool.com

Realidades ❶

Capítulo 5B

Nombre _____

Fecha _____

Hora _____

Practice Workbook **5B–5**

¿Quién viene?

Your class has decided to put on a talent show, and you are in charge of scheduling what time everyone is coming to audition for different skits. Your friend Lola is anxious to know the schedule. Answer her questions using the picture below. Follow the model.

Modelo   ¿Quién viene a las ocho y media?
La Sra. Ramos viene a las ocho y media.

1. ¿Quién viene a las nueve?

_____

2. ¿Quién viene a las diez?

_____

3. ¿Quién viene a las once menos cuarto?

_____

4. ¿Quién viene a las once y media?

_____

5. ¿Quién viene a las doce?

_____

6. ¿Quién viene a la una?

_____

7. ¿Quién viene a las dos y media?

_____

8. ¿Quién viene a las tres y media?

_____

Go Online WEB CODE jcd-0513
PHSchool.com

Una carta para mamá

Read the following letter from Rosaura to her mom in Spain. Write the form of **ser** or **estar** that best completes each sentence.

Querida mamá:

   ¡Aquí _____ en Chicago! Chicago _____ una gran ciudad

con muchas personas que _____ muy interesantes. La comida

_____ fantástica. La especialidad _____ la pizza. ¡Qué rica!

   Vivo con una familia muy simpática. Tienen un hijo que siempre

_____ contento y una hija que _____ muy estudiosa.

¡_____ las nueve de la noche y ella _____ en la biblioteca!

   Los chicos de la escuela también _____ estudiosos, pero no

muy serios. Mis compañeros y yo _____ muy buenos amigos y

_____ juntos todos los fines de semana. Una amiga, Vera,

_____ boliviana y _____ divertidísima. Vera y yo

_____ en la misma clase de biología.

   Bueno, mamá, _____ muy tarde. Mañana voy a _____

muy ocupada y necesito dormir. Pero sabes ahora que todo _____

bien aquí y que yo _____ contenta. Besos para ti y para papá.

                        Un abrazo,

                        Rosaura

Realidades ①

Capítulo 5B

Nombre _____

Fecha _____

Hora _____

Practice Workbook **5B–7**

¿Qué van a comer?

The Vázquez family is getting ready to order dinner in a restaurant. Look at the pictures to get an idea of the person's needs. Answer the questions below using vocabulary that would most logically go in each situation.

1.

¿Cómo está la Sra. Vázquez? _____

¿Qué debe pedir de plato principal? _____

¿De postre? _____ ¿Y para beber? _____

2.

¿Cómo están los chicos? _____

¿Qué deben pedir de plato principal? _____

¿De postre? _____ ¿Y para beber? _____

3.

¿Cómo está Elisita? _____

¿Qué debe pedir de plato principal? _____

¿De postre? _____ ¿Y para beber? _____

4.

¿Cómo está el Sr. Vázquez? _____

¿Qué debe pedir de plato principal? _____

¿De postre? _____ ¿Y para beber? _____

Go Online WEB CODE jcd-0515
PHSchool.com

Realidades ❶

Capítulo 5B

Nombre _____

Fecha _____

Hora _____

Practice Workbook **5B–8**

Repaso

Across

6. *blond;* el pelo ____

7. No bajo ____ .

8. Uds. ____ cansados.

12. Paquito no es viejo. Es ____ .

13. ¡Camarero, la ____ por favor!

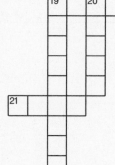

15.

16. Mi abuela tiene el pelo ____ .

17. Ella tiene 88 años. Es ____ .

18. Necesito un cuchillo y un ____ para comer el bistec.

19. sal y ____

21. Necesito un té. Tengo ____ .

Down

1. *red-haired (m.)*

2. El Sr. López es un ____ .

3. *napkin*

4. Nosotros ____ bajos.

5. *good-looking (f.)*

9. _____ el pelo ____

10. ¿Qué quieres de ____?
El flan.

11. Quiero un té helado. Tengo ____ .

13. no largo

14.

18. Quiero una ____ de café.

19. el plato ____

20. La Sra. Miranda es una ____ .

Organizer

I. Vocabulary

To describe people   **Things at a restaurant**

_____   _____

_____   _____

_____   _____

_____   _____

_____   _____

_____   _____

_____   _____

_____   **Words to describe how you're feeling**

Words to order food and beverages   _____

_____   _____

_____   _____

_____

_____

II. Grammar

1. The forms of **venir** are: _____   _____

   _____   _____

   _____   _____

2. For physical and personality descriptions, and to tell what time it is, use the verb

   _____. To talk about location and physical and emotional states,

   use the verb _____.

Go Online WEB CODE jcd-0516
PHSchool.com

Un dormitorio nuevo para mí

Ignacio is moving into his sister's room when she goes away to college. His parents have told him that he can bring anything into his new room that he can carry by himself. Make a list of eight things that he would definitely be able to bring with him, and five things that he definitely wouldn't be able to bring. Use the examples given to help you.

Traer conmigo

El lector DVD

_____

_____

_____

_____

_____

_____

_____

No traer conmigo

La pared

_____

_____

_____

_____

_____

Realidades ❶

Capítulo 6A

Nombre _____

Fecha _____

Hora _____

Practice Workbook **6A–2**

Muchos colores

Write the names of the color or colors that you associate with the following things. Don't forget to make the colors agree in gender and number.

1. el jugo de naranja _____ .

2. la limonada _____ .

3. el 14 de febrero _____ .

4. el 25 de diciembre _____ .

5. el sol _____ .

6. la nieve _____ .

7. unas zanahorias _____ .

8. la bandera de los Estados Unidos _____ .

9. un tomate _____ .

10. la piscina _____ .

11. la noche _____ .

12. el Día de San Patricio _____ .

Go Online WEB CODE jcd-0601
PHSchool.com

Realidades ❶

Capítulo 6A

Nombre _____

Hora _____

Fecha _____

Practice Workbook **6A–3**

La experiencia nueva

A. Read the letter that Gloria wrote to her friend in Spain about her host family in Chile.

> Querida Sandra,
>
> Lo paso muy bien aquí con la familia Quijano. Desde el primer día aquí, tengo mi propio dormitorio. Hay una cama, una mesita, una lámpara, un escritorio con una silla pequeña y un espejo. También hay una ventana con cortinas amarillas. La mejor cosa del cuarto es la lámpara. Es roja, negra y marrón y es muy artística. Creo que es la lámpara más bonita del mundo.
>
> El cuarto también es bonito. Las paredes son moradas. Sólo quiero mi equipo de sonido y mis discos compactos.
>
> Abrazos,
> *Gloria*

B. Now, answer these questions in complete sentences.

1. ¿A Gloria le gusta la familia?

_____

2. ¿Comparte Gloria el dormitorio con otro estudiante?

_____

3. ¿De qué color son las paredes en el dormitorio de Gloria?

_____

4. ¿Tiene Gloria su equipo de sonido en su dormitorio?

_____

5. ¿Cómo es la lámpara en el dormitorio de Gloria? ¿A ella le gusta?

_____

6. ¿De qué color son las cortinas en el dormitorio de Gloria?

Realidades ①

Capítulo 6A

Nombre _____

Fecha _____

Hora _____

Practice Workbook **6A–4**

¿Dónde está todo?

Movers just finished putting everything into Marcela's new room. Help her locate everything by describing where the items are in the picture below. Follow the model.

Modelo *Una lámpara está al lado del televisor.*

_____

_____

_____

_____

_____

_____

_____

Las comparaciones

Felipe and Mónica are brother and sister who are very different from each other. Using their pictures and the model to help you, write comparisons of the two siblings. Remember to make the adjectives agree in gender with the subject.

Modelo Mónica / alto *Mónica es más alta que Felipe.* _____

1. Felipe / serio _____

2. Mónica / sociable _____

3. Mónica / rubio _____

4. Felipe / estudioso _____

5. Felipe / alto _____

6. Mónica / viejo _____

7. Felipe / rubio _____

8. Felipe / joven _____

9. Mónica / serio _____

Los premios Óscar

The following chart rates movies according to certain categories. Four stars is the best rating, one star is the worst rating. Using the chart as a guide, write complete sentences comparing the three movies. Follow the model.

	Una tarde en agosto	*Mi vida*	*Siete meses en Lima*
Actores–talentosos	****	**	***
Fotografía–artística	****	*	***
Ropa–bonita	***	****	***
Director–creativo	****	***	**
Cuento–interesante	****	**	*

Modelo   actores / "Una tarde en agosto"

Los actores de Una tarde en agosto" son los más talentosos.

1. fotografía / "Una tarde en agosto"

_____

2. fotografía / "Mi vida"

_____

3. director / "Una tarde en agosto"

_____

4. actores / "Una tarde en agosto"

_____

5. director / "Siete meses en Lima"

_____

6. ropa / "Mi vida"

_____

7. cuento / "Siete meses en Lima"

_____

8. actores / "Mi vida"

_____

9. cuento / "Una tarde en agosto"

_____

Go Online WEB CODE jcd-0604
PHSchool.com

Las mini-conversaciones

A. Fill in the rest of these conjugations.

	DORMIR	PODER
yo		
tú		*puedes*
él, ella, Ud.	*duerme*	
nosotros		
vosotros	*dormís*	*podéis*
ellos, ellas, Uds.		

B. Write the correct forms of either **dormir** or **poder** in the blanks to complete the mini-conversations below.

1. —¿Quieres ir al cine?

   —No _____. Tengo que trabajar.

2. —¿Cuántas horas _____ cada noche?

   —Generalmente ocho horas.

3. —¿Uds. _____ venir a nuestra fiesta?

   —Sí. ¿A qué hora es?

4. —Nosotros no _____ trabajar hoy.

   —Está bien. Van a trabajar mañana.

5. —Cuando ellas van de cámping, ¿dónde _____?

   —Pues, en sus camas Coleman, por supuesto.

6. —¿Qué haces a las once y media de la noche?

   —¡Yo _____!

7. —¿_____ (tú) hablar con tu abuela por teléfono?

   —No, no _____ porque estoy ocupado.

8. —¿Qué hace una chica cansada?

   —_____ mucho.

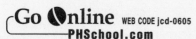

Realidades 1

Capítulo 6A

Nombre _____

Hora _____

Fecha _____

Practice Workbook **6A–8**

Repaso

Down ——————

1. Tengo que ____ por la noche.

2.

3. el ____ DVD

4. no pequeño

5.

6. un ____ compacto

8. no es a la derecha; es a la ____

11. Un plátano es de color ____.

13. *dresser*

17. La nieve es de color ____.

18. no mejor

Across ——————

2. Rojo y azul son ____.

7.

9.

10. el ____ de sonido

11. Hay una ____ debajo de la cama.

12. Uds. tienen mucha ropa en el ____.

14. Los libros están en el ____.

15. *brown*

16. no es fea, es ____

19. Duermo en la ____.

20. *mirror*

Organizer

I. Vocabulary

To talk about things in a bedroom

_____

_____

_____

_____

_____

_____

_____

Words to describe things

_____

_____

_____

_____

Electronic equipment

_____

_____

_____

_____

Words to talk about colors

_____

_____

_____

_____

_____

II. Grammar

1. To compare peoples' ages, use either _____ + **que** or _____ + **que**. To say that something is "better than" use _____ + **que**; to say that something is "worse than" use _____ + **que**.

2. To say that something is the "best" or "worst" use the following construction: article + _____ / _____ + noun. To say "most" or "least" the construction is article + noun + _____ / _____ + adjective.

3. The forms of **poder** are: The forms of **dormir** are:

_____ _____   _____ _____

_____ _____   _____ _____

_____ _____   _____ _____

Realidades ①

Capítulo 6B

Nombre _____

Fecha _____

Hora _____

Practice Workbook **6B–1**

Los cuartos

The Suárez family has just moved into a new house. Tell what rooms are on each floor of the house.

En la planta baja hay: _____

_____

_____

_____

En el primer piso hay: _____

_____

_____

_____

_____

Go Online
PHSchool.com WEB CODE jcd-0611

Los quehaceres

Each person below has been given a location from which to do his or her chores. In the spaces provided, list at least two chores each person could logically be doing. Follow the model.

Modelo   Alberto y Antonio están en el garaje.

lavan el coche

sacan la basura

limpian el garaje

1. Dolores está en el baño.

_____

_____

2. Eugenio está en el dormitorio.

_____

_____

_____

3. Carolina y Catarina están en la sala.

_____

_____

_____

4. Vladimir está en el comedor.

_____

_____

_____

5. Ana Gracia está en la cocina.

_____

_____

_____

La lista de quehaceres

Melisa's mom has left her a list of the things that she has to do before her relatives come over for a dinner party. Complete the list with the appropriate word or phrase. Follow the model.

Modelo _____*Arregla*_____ tu cuarto.

1. _____ la mesa del comedor.

2. Tienes que _____ porque no tienes ropa limpia.

3. _____ porque no tenemos platos limpios.

4. ¿Puedes _____? Hay demasiada basura.

5. _____ los platos en la cocina.

6. Necesitas _____ porque el coche está sucio.

7. Hay que _____ porque hay mucho polvo en el primer piso.

8. _____ las camas.

9. ¿Puedes _____ por las alfombras?

10. El baño no está limpio. Necesitas _____ .

11. _____ de comer al perro.

12. Si tienes tiempo, _____ todos los quehaceres.

Go Online WEB CODE jcd-0612
PHSchool.com

No es correcto

The following statements do not make sense. Rewrite the sentences by replacing the underlined words or phrases with words or phrases that make sense. Follow the model.

Modelo	Nunca <u>haces</u> en casa cuando tienes quehaceres.

Nunca ayudas en casa cuando tienes quehaceres _____.

1. Tengo que <u>dar</u> la aspiradora por las alfombras.

_____.

2. El cuarto está <u>limpio</u>. Voy a limpiarlo.

_____.

3. Papá va a lavar platos en <u>el dormitorio</u>.

_____.

4. No te <u>recibo</u> dinero porque no estás haciendo nada.

_____.

5. <u>¡Haz la cama!</u> Vamos a comer.

_____.

6. Mamá lava <u>el coche</u> en la cocina.

_____.

7. ¿Cuáles son los <u>dinero</u> que tienes que hacer?

_____.

8. Doy <u>dinero</u> al perro todos los días.

_____.

9. Debes cortar <u>el polvo</u>, está bastante largo.

_____.

10. Ernesto quita <u>el coche</u> de la sala.

_____.

11. Las hermanas <u>cocinan</u> la basura por la noche.

_____.

Los mandatos

A. Write the affirmative **tú** command forms of the following verbs in the spaces provided.

1. correr _____

2. poner _____

3. hacer _____

4. comer _____

5. hablar _____

6. leer _____

7. limpiar _____

8. ver _____

9. cortar _____

10. abrir _____

11. escribir _____

B. Now, write the chore your parents might tell you to do in each of the following situations. Follow the model.

Modelo Tu dormitorio no está limpio. *Arregla tu dormitorio* _____.

1. El coche está sucio. _____.

2. El perro tiene hambre. _____.

3. No hay platos limpios. _____.

4. Hay mucha basura en el garaje. _____.

5. La camisa blanca ahora es gris. _____.

6. Necesitamos cenar. _____.

7. El baño no está limpio. _____.

8. Hay mucho polvo en la sala. _____.

Go Online WEB CODE jcd-0613
PHSchool.com

Realidades ❶

Capítulo 6B

Nombre _____

Fecha _____

Hora _____

Practice Workbook **6B–6**

¿Qué están haciendo?

The Duarte family is getting ready for a barbecue. Look at the picture, then write what each of the family members is doing. Follow the model.

Modelo	La madre *está cocinando las hamburguesas* .

1. Manolo y José _____.

2. Ana María _____.

3. El padre _____.

4. Tito y Ramón _____.

5. Graciela _____.

6. Lola y Elia _____.

7. Todos _____.

Mucho trabajo

The Escobar family is getting ready to have guests over. Fill in the blanks in their conversation below with the appropriate form of the following verbs: **cortar, ayudar, hacer, lavar, pasar, sacar.**

PABLO: Mamá, ¿qué estás _____ tú?

MAMÁ: Estoy _____ los platos, hijo. ¿Y tú?

PABLO: Nada.

MAMÁ: Vale. ¿Qué están _____ tus hermanos?

PABLO: Juan está _____ el baño y Marta está arreglando

su dormitorio.

MAMÁ: Bien, hijo. Ahora, quita el polvo de la sala y luego _____

la aspiradora por las alfombras.

PABLO: Pero, mamá …

MAMÁ: ¡Ahora! Y después _____ la basura …

¡María! ¿Qué estás _____ , hija?

MARÍA: Isabel y yo _____ el césped. ¿Por qué?

MAMÁ: Porque tus primos vienen a comer hoy y necesito ayuda para poner la mesa.

MARIA: ¿Por qué no te está _____ papá?

MAMÁ: Papá, cariño, ¿dónde estás?

PAPÁ: Estoy en el garaje. Estoy _____ el coche.

MAMÁ: Ah, sí. Después, arregla nuestro cuarto y _____ tu ropa sucia.

PAPÁ: ¿Por qué?

MAMÁ: ¡Vienen tu hermano y su familia!

Go Online WEB CODE jcd-0615
PHSchool.com

Realidades

Capítulo 6B

Nombre _____

Fecha _____

Hora _____

Practice Workbook **6B-8**

Repaso

Across

4. cómo pasas al primer piso desde la planta baja; la ____

6. Yo ____ el baño

9.

12. *to cook*

15. El hijo ____ la aspiradora cada fin de semana.

16.

____ el cuarto

17. La hija debe ____ los platos ahora.

18. un cuarto donde puedes poner el coche

20. cuarto donde come la familia; el ____

21. el piso más bajo de la casa

Down

1. el cuarto donde preparas la comida

2. Tengo que ____ la cama hoy.

3.

quitar el ____

5.

____ la basura

6. no cerca

7. Después de subir la escalera, estás en el ____.

8. Cuando entras en la casa, estás en la ____ ____.

10. la oficina en la casa

11. ¿Quién va a ____ la mesa?

13. el cuarto donde ves la tele

14. el cuarto donde duermes

19. Mateo tiene que cortar el ____.

21. no limpio

Organizer

I. Vocabulary

Rooms of the house

_____

_____

_____

_____

_____

_____

_____

Outdoor chores

_____

_____

_____

_____

Indoor household tasks

_____

_____

_____

_____

_____

Floors of the house

_____

_____

_____

_____

II. Grammar

1. To talk about actions in progress, use the _____ tense.

   This is formed by adding -_____ to the roots of **-ar** verbs and -_____

   to the roots of **-er** and **-ir** verbs.

2. **Tú** commands are the same as the _____ form of the

   _____ tense of verbs. But the **tú** command form of **poner** is

   _____ and of **hacer** is _____.

Go Online WEB CODE jcd-0616
PHSchool.com

Realidades ①

Capítulo 7A

Nombre _____

Hora _____

Fecha _____

Practice Workbook **7A–1**

En el escaparate (*store window*)

You are window shopping at a large department store and you decide to make a list of what they have and what everything costs. Using the picture, list seven items and their prices below. Follow the model.

| Modelo | *Los pantalones cuestan 35 dólares.* |

1. _____

2. _____

3. _____

4. _____

5. _____

6. _____

7. _____

Tienda de la Gracia

A. Write the numbers below in Spanish.

1. 100 _____

2. 500 _____

3. 909 _____

4. 222 _____

5. 767 _____

6. 676 _____

7. 110 _____

8. 881 _____

B. Read the following statistics about the chain of stores **Tienda de la Gracia**. Then answer the questions that follow.

TIENDA DE LA GRACIA	
Tiendas	100
Trabajadores	324
Promedio diario (*daily average*) de clientes	760
Camisas	612
Pantalones	404

1. ¿Cuántas Tiendas de la Gracia hay?

_____

2. ¿Cuál es el promedio diario de clientes en cada tienda?

_____

3. ¿Cuántos trabajadores hay en las Tiendas de la Gracia?

_____

4. ¿Cuántos pantalones hay en cada tienda?

_____

5. ¿Y camisas?

_____

Go Online WEB CODE jcd-0701
PHSchool.com

En el centro comercial

Tatiana and Mariana are in the local mall. Write the words that most logically complete their conversation as they go from store to store.

TATIANA: Vamos a esta tienda de ropa. Aquí tienen _____ elegante.

MARIANA: Bien. ¿Qué _____ comprar?

TATIANA: Necesito un vestido para la fiesta de mi primo.

DEPENDIENTA: ¿En qué puedo _____, señorita?

TATIANA: _____ un vestido elegante.

DEPENDIENTA: ¿Va Ud. a _____ el vestido a una fiesta o un baile formal?

TATIANA: A una fiesta. Me gusta este vestido.

MARIANA: ¿Cómo te _____?

TATIANA: ¡Me queda fantástico! Quiero comprarlo.

MARIANA: Vamos a otra tienda. Necesito _____ unos zapatos nuevos. Vamos a esa tienda, tienen buenos precios allí.

TATIANA: Mira estos zapatos aquí.

MARIANA: ¿Cuánto cuestan?

TATIANA: Trescientos dólares. ¿Es un buen _____?

MARIANA: Sí. Y me quedan _____. Voy a comprar estos zapatos.

TATIANA: Bien. Pasamos a otra tienda.

MARIANA: La tienda de música está a la derecha. ¿Entramos?

TATIANA: Sí, ¡ _____!

Realidades

Capítulo 7A

Nombre _____

Hora _____

Fecha _____

Practice Workbook **7A–4**

¿Qué llevan?

In complete sentences, describe two articles of clothing that each of the people below is wearing.

Pedro

A. _____

_____

B. _____

_____

1.

Las hermanas Guzmán

A. _____

_____

B. _____

_____

2.

La profesora Jones

A. _____

_____

B. _____

_____

3.

El Dr. Cambambia

A. _____

_____

B. _____

_____

4.

Anita

A. _____

_____

B. _____

_____

5.

Go Online WEB CODE jcd-0702
PHSchool.com

Realidades ❶

Capítulo 7A

Nombre _____

Fecha _____

Hora _____

Practice Workbook **7A–5**

Algunos verbos nuevos

A. Fill in the chart below with the forms of the stem-changing verbs indicated.

	PENSAR	QUERER	PREFERIR
yo	*pienso*		
tú			*prefieres*
él, ella, Ud.		*quiere*	
nosotros			*preferimos*
vosotros	*pensáis*	*queréis*	*preferís*
ellos, ellas, Uds.		*quieren*	

B. Now, complete each sentence below by choosing the correct form of the verb **pensar**, **querer**, or **preferir**.

1. ¿ _____ (tú) la camisa roja o la camisa azul?

2. Nosotros _____ comprar un suéter nuevo.

3. Ellas _____ ir de compras hoy.

4. Vivian _____ llevar ropa elegante.

5. ¿Uds. _____ trabajar en la tienda de Mónica?

6. Yo _____ comprar los zapatos ahora.

7. Mis amigos y yo _____ jugar al fútbol cuando llueve.

8. Eduardo _____ ir a la fiesta con Brenda.

9. ¿Qué _____ (tú) hacer después de la escuela?

10. Marcelo y Claudio _____ ir al gimnasio después de la escuela.

11. Yo _____ buscar una bicicleta nueva.

12. ¿Tomás va a la tienda o _____ quedarse en casa?

¿Cuál prefieres?

A. Fill in the chart below with the singular and plural, masculine and feminine forms of the demonstrative adjectives.

este		estos	
	esa		esas

B. Complete the following questions about the clothing items pictured by writing in the appropriate demonstrative adjectives from the chart above. Then answer the questions by saying that you prefer the item indicated by the arrow.

1. —¿Prefieres _____ camisa o _____ suéter?

—_____

—_____

2. —¿Prefieres _____ pantalones cortos o _____ jeans?

—_____

—_____

3. —¿Te gustan más _____ sudaderas aquí o _____ suéteres?

—_____

—_____

4. —¿Te gusta más _____ vestido o _____ falda?

—_____

—_____

5. —¿Quieres _____ zapatos negros o _____ botas negras?

—_____

—_____

6. —¿Prefieres _____ chaqueta o _____ abrigo?

—_____

—_____

Go Online WEB CODE jcd-0703
PHSchool.com

¿Quién?

Two sales associates are discussing some of the clients in their busy store. Fill in the blanks with the appropriate demonstrative adjectives based on the picture.

CELIA: ¿Qué hace _____ mujer allá?

YOLANDA: Pues, está mirando las botas, pero no quiere pagar mucho.

CELIA: ¿Qué quieren _____ mujeres aquí?

YOLANDA: Piensan comprar unos calcetines.

CELIA: ¿Y _____ hombre solo allí?

YOLANDA: ¿_____ hombre? Prefiere mirar los pantalones.

CELIA: A la derecha de él hay unos niños, ¿no? ¿Qué hacen _____ niños?

YOLANDA: Pues, _____ niños quieren unos suéteres nuevos.

CELIA: Oye, ¿ves a _____ hombres al lado de la puerta?

YOLANDA: Sí, piensan comprar _____ abrigos. ¿Por qué?

CELIA: Pues, son muy guapos, ¿no?

YOLANDA: Ah, sí. Creo que necesitan ayuda.

CELIA: ¡Hasta luego!

Realidades ❶

Capítulo 7A

Nombre _____

Hora _____

Fecha _____

Practice Workbook **7A–8**

Repaso

Down —————————

1.

2.

4. ¿Cuánto ____ las botas?

5. Mi padre es inteligente. Siempre tiene ____.

6. 5000 ÷ 10

8. ____, señorita. Necesito ayuda.

9. Llevo una ____ en la cabeza.

11. Cuando hace frío, llevo un ____.

13. la ____ de ropa

16. 500 x 2

Across —————————

2. Llevas ____ debajo de los zapatos.

3. ____ de baño

6. ¿Te ____ bien ese suéter?

7.

8. los ____ cortos

10. Yo llevo ____ en los pies.

12. No cuestan tanto. Es un buen ____.

14. En esta tienda, quiero ____ unas botas.

15. Jaime es informal. Siempre lleva camiseta y los ____.

17. Ella tiene que comprar un ____ para la fiesta.

18.

Realidades 1

Capítulo 7A

Nombre _____

Hora _____

Fecha _____

Practice Workbook **7A–9**

Organizer

I. Vocabulary

Clothing for warm weather

_____

_____

_____

_____

_____

Clothing for cold weather

_____

_____

_____

_____

_____

_____

Other words to talk about clothing

_____

_____

_____

Numbers in the hundreds

_____

_____

_____

_____

_____

_____

II. Grammar

1. The forms of the verb **pensar** are: _____ _____

   _____ _____

   _____ _____

   The forms of the verb **querer** are: _____ _____

   _____ _____

   _____ _____

   The forms of the verb **preferir** are: _____ _____

   _____ _____

   _____ _____

2. To refer to something close, use _____ / _____, _____ / _____; to refer to something further away, use _____ / _____, _____ / _____.

Realidades ①

Capítulo 7B

Nombre _____

Hora _____

Fecha _____

Practice Workbook **7B–1**

Los regalos

Marcela is writing a list of gifts she wants to buy for her family. Help her by writing the names of the items suggested by the pictures in the blanks provided.

1. Para mi novio:

_____ _____ _____ _____

2. Para mi mejor amiga:

_____ _____

3. Para mi hermana:

_____ _____ _____ _____

4. Para mi padre:

_____ _____ _____

5. Para mi madre:

_____ _____ _____

Go Online WEB CODE jcd-0711
PHSchool.com

¡Tantas tiendas!

Write the names of the items pictured in the first blank, and where each person would find the items in the second blank.

1. Yo busco _____

    en una _____.

2. Germán busca _____

    en una _____.

3. Tú buscas _____

    en la _____.

4. Mi hermano busca _____

    en la _____.

5. Bárbara busca _____

    en un _____.

6. Buscamos _____

    en la _____.

7. Esteban y Luis buscan un _____

    en la _____.

8. Susana y Paulina buscan _____

    en una _____.

9. —¿En dónde puedo comprar _____?

    —En un _____.

¿El regalo perfecto?

Valentine's Day is coming and Pepe and Laura are deciding what gifts to give each other.

A. Read the conversations below.

    (*En una tienda de descuentos*)
PEPE: Necesito comprar un regalo para mi novia.
DEPENDIENTE: ¿Qué piensa comprar?
PEPE: No sé. Tiene que ser algo barato porque no tengo mucho dinero.
DEPENDIENTE: Pero, ¿no quiere un anillo bonito o un collar elegante para su novia?
PEPE: No. Es demasiado.
DEPENDIENTE: Puede comprar un reloj pulsera que no cuesta tanto.
PEPE: Oiga, el mes pasado compré software nuevo para mi computadora, para poder jugar videojuegos en la Red. ¡Pagué unos 90 dólares!
DEPENDIENTE: Entonces quiere este llavero de veinte dólares.
PEPE: ¡Genial!

    (*En un almacén*)
LAURA: Quiero el regalo perfecto para mi novio.
DEPENDIENTA: ¿Él trabaja? ¿Quizás una corbata bonita?
LAURA: Estoy pensando en un regalo más romántico . . .
DEPENDIENTA: ¿Unos guantes para las noches de frío?
LAURA: No creo. Él nunca tiene frío. ¿Ud. tiene algo romántico?
DEPENDIENTA: ¡Mire! ¿Qué piensa de este anillo de cincuenta dólares?
LAURA: ¡Perfecto! Quiero uno, por favor.

B. Answer the questions about the dialogues in complete sentences.

1. ¿A qué tienda va Pepe? _____

    ¿Qué busca allí? ¿Por qué? _____

2. ¿Qué quiere venderle el dependiente? ¿Por qué Pepe no quiere comprarlos? _____

3. ¿Qué compra por fin Pepe? _____

4. ¿Qué quiere comprar Laura? _____

5. ¿Por qué Laura no quiere ni una corbata ni unos guantes? _____

6. ¿Qué va a comprar Laura? _____ ¿Es más caro o más barato que el regalo de Pepe? _____

Go Online WEB CODE jcd-0712 PHSchool.com

Oraciones desordenadas

Put the scrambled sentences below into logical order.

1. compré / hace / lo / semana / una

_____

2. yo / por / ayer / unos / pagué / un / guantes / dólar

_____

3. lector / caro / DVD / un / es / muy / no

_____

4. joyas / en / venden / almacén / el

_____

5. pasada / la / compré / yo / semana / suéter / nuevo / un

_____

6. anoche / una / compré / computadora / yo / nueva

_____

7. pagaste / el / collar / cuánto / por

¿_____?

8. lo / año / el / tú / compraste / pasado

_____

9. joyas / por / venden / tienda / esta / veinte / en / dólares

_____

10. cuánto / por / el / pagaste / reloj

¿_____?

Hablamos del pasado

A. Fill in the chart below with the preterite forms of the verbs indicated.

	COMPRAR	HABLAR	PREPARAR	USAR	MIRAR
yo	compré				
tú					miraste
él, ella, Ud.		habló			
nosotros				usamos	
vosotros	comprasteis	hablasteis	preparasteis	usasteis	mirasteis
ellos, ellas, Uds.			prepararon		

B. Fill in the blanks in the following postcard with the correct preterite forms of the verbs given.

¡Hola, mamá!

 ¿Cómo estás? Estoy muy bien aquí en Quito.
Primero, José y yo _____ (preparar) unos
sándwiches ricos y _____ (hablar) con su
mamá un poco. Después, decidimos ir al centro
comercial. José y su mamá _____ (mirar)
unas chaquetas en la tienda de Smith y yo
_____ (comprar) algunas cosas para la
semana.

 A las cinco, la mamá de José _____
(llamar) por teléfono al padre, y él _____
(regresar) del trabajo un poco después. Nosotros
_____ (cenar) y _____ (usar) la
computadora antes de dormir.

 ¿Y tú? ¿_____ (caminar) esta semana?
¿_____ (comprar) el regalo para el
cumpleaños de papi? Pues, nos vemos en una semana.
¡Mañana me voy a Lima!

 Un abrazo,
 Víctor

La Sra. Guiraldo
Vía Águila 1305
Col. Cuauhtémoc
06500 México, D.F.

ECUADOR 40

WEB CODE jcd-0713
PHSchool.com

Realidades ①

Capítulo 7B

Nombre _____

Hora _____

Fecha _____

Practice Workbook **7B–6**

Mini-conversaciones

A. Fill in the following charts with the preterite forms of the verbs given.

	PAGAR	**BUSCAR**	**JUGAR**	**PRACTICAR**	**TOCAR**
yo	*pagué*			*practiqué*	
tú			*jugaste*		
él, ella, Ud.		*buscó*			
nosotros					*tocamos*
vosotros	*pagasteis*	*buscasteis*	*jugasteis*	*practicasteis*	*tocasteis*
ellos, ellas, Uds.				*practicaron*	

B. Now, complete the mini-conversations below with preterite verb forms from the chart above.

1. —Juan, ¿cuánto _____ por tu suéter?

   —Yo _____ 25 dólares.

2. —¿Qué hizo Marta anoche?

   —Ella _____ al fútbol con sus hermanos.

3. —Hija, ¿_____ el piano?

   —Sí, mamá. _____ por una hora.

4. —Busco un apartamento nuevo.

   —Yo _____ por un año antes de encontrar el apartamento perfecto.

5. —¿Uds. _____ un instrumento en el pasado?

   —Sí, nosotros _____ el violín.

6. —¿Marcos va a practicar el básquetbol hoy?

   —No, él _____ toda la semana pasada.

7. —¿Con quién _____ (tú) al golf?

   —_____ con mis dos hermanos y con mi padre.

WEB CODE jcd-0714

Manos a la obra ━ *Gramática* **135**

Objeto directo

A. Rewrite the following sentences about shopping using direct object pronouns in place of the appropriate nouns.

1. Compré los zapatos. _____

2. ¿Tienes el vestido verde? _____

3. Escribo el cuento. _____

4. Mi mamá recibe el dinero. _____

5. Las mujeres llevan las faldas nuevas. _____

6. ¿Rosario va a comprar el regalo? _____

7. Las amigas compraron aretes nuevos. _____

8. Llevo los dos abrigos. _____

B. Ramona's mother is talking to her about their trip to the mall. Answer her questions using direct object pronouns. Follow the model.

Modelo   ¿Llevas tu vestido nuevo a la escuela?

Sí, lo llevo mucho. _____

1. ¿Dónde vas a poner tu camisa nueva?

   _____

2. ¿Compraste los zapatos azules?

   _____

3. ¿Usas el reloj pulsera negro?

   _____

4. ¿Cuándo vas a llevar tus guantes nuevos?

   _____

5. ¿Tienes las camisetas nuevas?

   _____

Go Online WEB CODE jcd-0715
PHSchool.com

Repaso

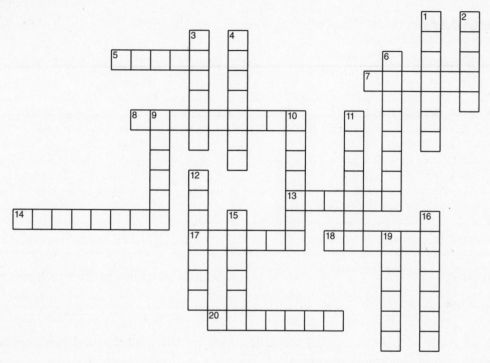

Across ─────────────

5. donde las mujeres ponen las llaves, bolígrafos, etc.
7. la ___ de electrodomésticos
8. tienda donde venden zapatos

13.
14. los ___ de sol
17. Una tienda de ropa es donde ___ ropa.
18. no caro
20. tienda donde venden joyas

Down ─────────────

1. Llevo los ___ durante el invierno porque tengo las manos frías.
2. Sancho quiere ___ las fotos de tu viaje.

3.
4. donde pones el dinero y a veces unas fotos; la ___
6. tienda donde venden libros
9. joya que llevas en las orejas
10. tienda donde venden todo
11. tipo de reloj que llevas en el cuerpo; reloj ___
12. donde pones las llaves
15. joya que llevas en el dedo
16. Los hombres llevan una camisa con ___ al trabajo.
19. *last night*

Organizer

I. Vocabulary

Types of stores

_____
_____
_____
_____
_____
_____

Words to talk about jewelry

_____
_____
_____
_____
_____
_____

Other gifts

_____
_____
_____
_____

Words to talk about the past

_____
_____
_____
_____

II. Grammar

1. The preterite endings of **-ar** verbs are: -_____   -_____
   -_____   -_____
   -_____   -_____

   Now conjugate the verb **pasar** in the preterite: _____   _____

   _____   _____

   _____   _____

2. The preterite ending of the **yo** form of verbs ending with **-car** is -_____. For
   -gar verbs it is -_____.

3. The direct object pronouns are _____, _____, _____, and

   _____.

Go Online WEB CODE jcd-0717
PHSchool.com

Realidades ❶

Capítulo 8A

Nombre _____

Hora _____

Fecha _____

Practice Workbook **8A–1**

¿Adónde van?

Complete the mini-conversations. Use the drawing to fill in the first blank and to give you a clue for the second blank. Follow the model.

Modelo

—¿Viste el ___monumento___ nuevo de Cristóbal Colón?

—Sí, ¡es fantástico! Está enfrente del ___museo___.

1. —Mamá, quiero ver _____.

—Sí, Marisol. Vamos al _____.

2. —¿Uds. van de vacaciones en _____ este verano?

—No, vamos a la _____.

3. —¿Vas a ver _____ hoy?

—Sí, mis padres y yo vamos al _____.

4. —¿Quieres _____ hoy?

—Sí, pero ¿en dónde? ¿En el _____?

5. —¿Dónde es el _____?

—Pues, en el _____, por supuesto.

6. —¿Cómo te gusta ir de _____?

—Siempre viajamos en _____.

Asociaciones

A. Write the names of the places from your vocabulary that you associate with the following things or actions.

1. la historia, el arte ___ ___ ___ ◯ ___ ___ ___ ___ ◯

2. las atracciones, los monos ___ ___ ___ ◯ ___ ___ ___ ___ ___

3. pintar, dibujar, el arte ___ ___ ◯ ___ ___ ___

4. divertido, personas atrevidas, jugar ___ ___ ◯ ___ ___ ___ ___

    ___ ___ ___ ___ ◯ ___ ___ ___ ___ ◯

5. los deportes, un partido, ver ◯ ___ ___ ___ ◯ ___ ___

6. la obra, el actor ___ ◯ ___ ___ ___ ___ ___

7. el hotel, muchas personas ◯ ___ ___ ___ ___ ___ ___

8. pasear en bote, mucha agua ___ ___ ___ ◯

B. Now, unscramble the circled letters to find a related word.

___ ___ ___   ___ ___ ___ ___ ___ ___ ___

Go Online WEB CODE jcd-0801
PHSchool.com

¡Vamos al parque nacional!

The Carreras family went on vacation to Rocky Mountain National Park in Colorado. Read the postcard they sent to their friends back home and fill in the blanks with the words suggested by the pictures.

¡Saludos desde Colorado!

Llegamos al _____ el lunes pasado. Yo fui directamente

a la playa para _____ . El _____

es precioso y ¡los _____ son enormes! El martes paseamos

en _____ por el lago y miramos los _____

_____ . ¡Yo vi un oso en el bosque!

Para mañana tenemos muchos planes. Vamos a _____

por las montañas y por la noche vamos al _____ para ver

una obra musical.

Regresamos a la _____ el viernes. ¡Nos vemos

este fin de semana!

           Abrazos,

           Familia Carreras

Realidades (1)

Capítulo 8A

Nombre _____

Fecha _____

Hora _____

Practice Workbook **8A–4**

¿Qué te pasó?

A. Read the dialogue between Aníbal and Carmen about Aníbal's trip to the beach.

CARMEN: Dime, ¿fuiste a la playa con tus primos?

ANÍBAL: ¡Ay, amiga; fue un desastre! Salí muy temprano para pasar todo el día allí.

Durante el día tomamos el sol y buceamos en el mar.

CARMEN: ¿No fue un día tremendo para descansar y pasarlo bien con tus amigos?

ANÍBAL: Por dos horas, sí. Pero después de mucha lluvia, todo salió mal.

CARMEN: Lo siento. Va a hacer buen tiempo este sábado. . .

ANÍBAL: Bueno, tú y yo podemos salir de la ciudad.

CARMEN: ¡Genial!

B. Now, answer the questions in complete sentences.

1. ¿Adónde fue Aníbal? _____

_____

2. ¿Qué hizo allí? _____

_____

3. ¿Con quién fue Aníbal? _____

_____

4. ¿Qué tiempo va a hacer el sábado? _____

_____

5. ¿Qué van a hacer Aníbal y Carmen? _____

_____

Go Online WEB CODE jcd-0802
PHSchool.com

Realidades ❶

Capítulo 8A

Nombre _____

Hora _____

Fecha _____

Practice Workbook **8A–5**

¿Qué hicieron?

A. Fill in the chart with the preterite forms of the verbs given.

	COMER	ESCRIBIR	CORRER	SALIR	VER	BEBER
yo	comí				vi	
tú			corriste			
él, ella, Ud.				salió		bebió
nosotros		escribimos				
vosotros	comisteis	escribisteis	corristeis	salisteis	visteis	bebisteis
ellos/as, Uds.						

B. Now, complete the mini-conversations below by filling in the appropriate forms of one of the verbs from Part A.

1. —Pablo, ¿vas a correr hoy?

    —No, _____ ayer.

2. —¿Elena _____ toda
    la leche?

    —Sí, toda.

3. —¿Uds. salieron anoche?

    —Sí, _____ a las once.

4. —¿_____ la nueva
    película de Almodóvar?

    —Sí, la vi anoche.

5. —¡Qué buenos niños!

    —Sí, _____ todas las
    zanahorias.

6. —Juan, escribe la tarea.

    —Ya la _____ , mamá.

7. —¿Uds. comieron en el hotel anoche?

    —No, _____ en el
    restaurante.

8. —¿Quién va a correr en el maratón
    este año?

    —Todos, porque sólo dos personas

    _____ el año pasado.

9. —¿Con quién saliste, Marta?

    —_____ con Toño.

10. —¿El autor va a escribir un cuento
    nuevo?

    —No, él _____ uno el mes
    pasado.

WEB CODE jcd-0803

Manos a la obra ➖ *Gramática* **143**

Realidades ①

Capítulo 8A

Nombre _____

Hora _____

Fecha _____

Practice Workbook **8A–6**

¿Adónde fueron?

Some friends are talking about where they went on vacation. Write where they went, using the pictures below to help you. Follow the model.

Modelo La familia Madrigal *fue al zoológico* _____.

1. Carlos _____.

2. Yo _____.

3. Lola y Tina _____.

4. Nosotros _____.

5. Elisa _____.

6. Tú _____.

7. Uds. _____.

Go Online WEB CODE jcd-0804
PHSchool.com

Realidades 1

Capítulo 8A

Nombre _____

Fecha _____

Hora _____

Practice Workbook **8A–7**

¿Qué viste?

Alicia saw many things at the park yesterday. Use the drawing and the location clues to say whom or what she saw. Pay attention to the use of the personal **a** in your statements. Follow the model.

Modelo   En el parque ayer, yo vi ___*a unos amigos*___ corriendo.

1. Yo vi _____ dándoles de comer a unos pájaros.

2. Yo vi _____ jugando al fútbol.

3. Yo vi _____ en la mesa.

4. En el lago, yo vi _____ paseando.

5. En el bote, yo vi _____ con una señorita.

6. En un árbol yo vi _____.

7. Al lado del árbol vi _____.

8. Debajo del árbol vi _____ con pelo largo.

9. En la playa vi _____.

Realidades 1

Capítulo 8A

Nombre _____

Hora _____

Fecha _____

Practice Workbook **8A–8**

Repaso

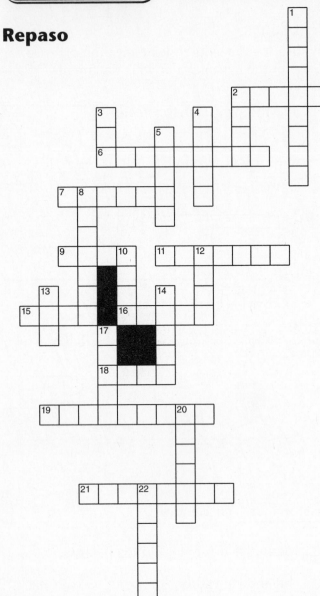

Down

1. Me gusta ___ en el sofá.
2. donde puedes pasear en bote; el ___
3. Yo quiero ___ la tele.
4. medio de transporte que va por el agua; el ___
5. un edificio con muchos cuadros; el ___
8. medio de transporte que usan los estudiantes para ir a la escuela; el ___
10. la ___ de teatro
12. *the train*; el ___
13. *the sea*; el ___
14. sinónimo de **vacaciones**; un ___

17.
20. Chicago es una ___ donde hace mucho viento.

22.

Across

2. *place*; un ___
6. En el monumento, compramos ___.
7. el ___ de diversiones

9.

11. donde se juegan los partidos de fútbol; el ___
15. España es un ___ donde hablan español.
16. medio de transporte que va por el aire; el ___
18. pasear en ___
19. donde hay atracciones de animales; el ___
21. no tarde

Realidades ①

Capítulo 8A

Nombre _____ Hora _____

Fecha _____ Practice Workbook **8A–9**

Organizer

I. Vocabulary

Places to visit

_____

_____

_____

_____

_____

Modes of transportation

_____

_____

_____

_____

_____

Leisure activities

_____

_____

_____

_____

Phrases to discuss experiences

_____

_____

_____

_____

II. Grammar

1. The preterite endings of **-er** and **-ir** verbs are:

    yo   -_____   nosotros -_____

    tú   -_____   vosotros -_isteis_____

    Ud. -_____   Uds.   -_____

2. The preterite forms of **ir** (and **ser**) are: _____ _____

    _____ _____

    _____ _____

3. _____ is inserted before the direct object of a sentence if the direct object

    is a person. This is called the _____.

Realidades ①

Capítulo 8B

Nombre _____

Hora _____

Fecha _____

Practice Workbook **8B–1**

La comunidad

Your new friend in Costa Rica is showing you around her community. Label each place or point of interest in the picture with the appropriate word.

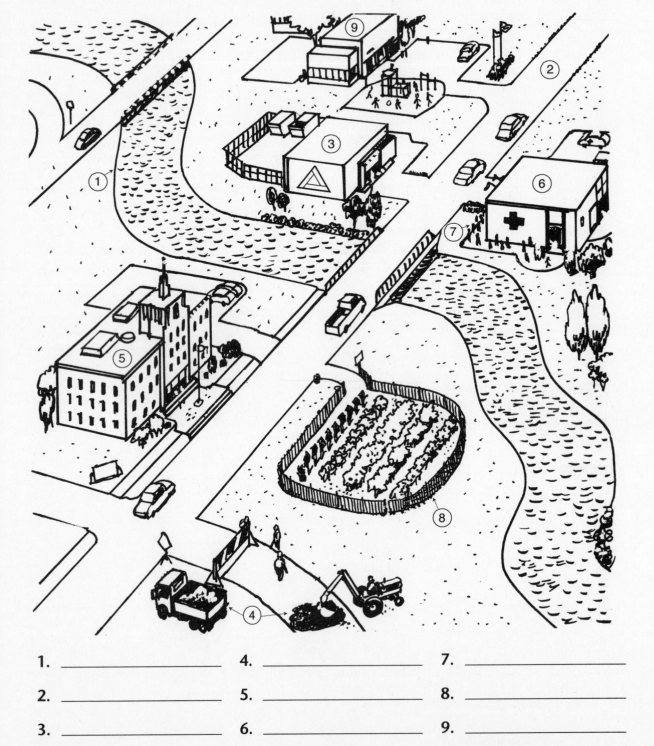

1. _____   4. _____   7. _____

2. _____   5. _____   8. _____

3. _____   6. _____   9. _____

Go Online   WEB CODE jcd-0811
PHSchool.com

Realidades ①

Capítulo 8B

Nombre _____

Fecha _____

Hora _____

Practice Workbook **8B–2**

El reciclaje

A. Your community is starting a recycling program. Label each item below with words from your vocabulary.

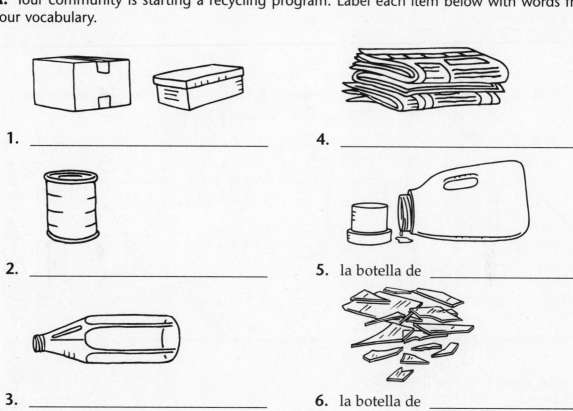

1. _____

2. _____

3. _____

4. _____

5. la botella de _____

6. la botella de _____

B. Now, write sentences to say whether or not it is necessary to recycle the items below. Follow the model.

Modelo Los tomates *No es necesario reciclar los tomates.* _____

1. El helado _____

2. El plástico _____

3. El vidrio _____

4. La sala _____

5. Las latas _____

Realidades 1

Capítulo 8B

Nombre _____

Fecha _____

Hora _____

Practice Workbook **8B–3**

El voluntario

A. Read the letter below from Álvaro, who is working as an AmeriCorps volunteer.

Querida familia:

¡Qué experiencia! Hacemos tantas cosas para ayudar a los demás. La semana pasada ayudamos en un proyecto de construcción con otro grupo de voluntarios. Ellos van a terminar el proyecto. Después de eso, fuimos a un centro de reciclaje. Allí aprendimos a reciclar el papel y el vidrio. También nos enseñaron cómo separar el papel normal (como el papel de los libros) de los periódicos.

Esta semana nosotros recogimos mucha ropa usada de varias partes de la ciudad y la llevamos a un centro para pobres. Allí le dimos la ropa a la gente pobre del barrio.

Hoy vamos a un centro para ancianos para ayudar a personas mayores. Estoy cansado, pero es importante hacer esto.

¡Hasta pronto!

Álvaro

B. Now, answer the questions below.

1. ¿Cuántas cosas hace Álvaro para ayudar a los demás? ¿Cuáles son? _____

_____

2. ¿Qué aprendió Álvaro en el centro de reciclaje? _____

_____

3. ¿Adónde llevaron Álvaro y los voluntarios la ropa usada? _____

_____

4. ¿A quiénes le dieron la ropa? _____

_____

5. ¿Qué hace Álvaro hoy? _____

_____

Go Online WEB CODE jcd-0812 PHSchool.com

Realidades 1

Capítulo 8B

Nombre _____

Fecha _____

Hora _____

Practice Workbook **8B-4**

¿Qué haces en la comunidad?

You overhear two friends telling their teacher about what they do to help out in their communities. You can't hear what the teacher is asking. Fill in the teacher's questions. Follow the model.

Modelo   —*¿Uds. ayudan en la comunidad?*

        —Sí, trabajamos como voluntarios en la comunidad.

—¿ _____ ?

—Trabajamos en una escuela primaria. Les enseñamos a los niños a leer.

—¿ _____ ?

—También recogemos ropa usada.

—¿ _____ ?

—Recogemos la ropa usada del barrio.

—¿ _____ ?

—Hay que separar la ropa y después lavarla.

—¿ _____ ?

—Le damos la ropa usada a la gente pobre del barrio.

—¿ _____ ?

—Sí, ayudamos en el hospital.

—¿ _____ ?

—Trabajamos como voluntarios en un hospital para niños. Nos encanta el trabajo voluntario.

¿Quién dice qué?

The people in the chart below are concerned citizens. Tell what each says by combining the subject on the left with the phrase on the right using **decir** + **que**. Follow the model.

Subjects	Phrases
Smokey the Bear	Hay que tener cuidado en el campamento.
Los directores del centro de reciclaje	Es necesario separar el plástico y el vidrio.
Gloria	La gente tiene que limpiar el barrio.
Yo	Todos deben participar en las actividades de la comunidad.
La profesora	Es esencial hacer trabajo voluntario.
La Cruz Roja	Es importante ayudar a los enfermos.
Tú	Es importante llevar la ropa usada a centros para los pobres.
Mi familia y yo	Es importante reciclar las botellas y latas.

Modelo   *Smokey the Bear dice que hay que tener cuidado en el campamento.*

1. _____

2. _____

3. _____

4. _____

5. _____

6. _____

7. _____

Go Online WEB CODE jcd-0813
PHSchool.com

Más trabajo voluntario

A. Write the indirect object pronouns that correspond to the following phrases.

1. A Javier y a Sara _____
2. A Diego y a mí _____
3. A la Dra. Estes _____
4. A Uds. _____
5. A Tito _____

6. A Luz y a ti _____
7. A ti _____
8. A nosotros _____
9. Al Sr. Pérez _____
10. A mí _____

B. Now, fill in the blanks in the following sentences with the correct indirect object pronouns.

1. La Cruz Roja _____ ayuda a las personas de la comunidad.

2. Nuestros padres _____ hablaron a mi hermano y a mí del reciclaje.

3. Mi profesora _____ ayudó a decidir qué trabajo voluntario me gustaría hacer.

4. _____ dice el profesor al estudiante que es importante separar las latas y el plástico.

5. Las personas _____ escriben al director del centro de reciclaje para recibir información sobre el reciclaje.

6. ¿Tus padres _____ dicen que debes ayudar a los demás?

7. _____ traigo unos juguetes a los niños en el hospital.

8. Los ancianos están muy contentos cuando _____ decimos que volvemos mañana.

Realidades ①

Capítulo 8B

Nombre _____

Fecha _____

Hora _____

Practice Workbook **8B–7**

¿Hacer o dar?

A. Fill in the chart below with the correct forms of **hacer** and **dar** in the preterite.

	HACER	DAR
yo	hice	di
tú		
él, ella, Ud.		
nosotros		
vosotros	hicisteis	disteis
ellos, ellas, Uds.		

B. Now, fill in the blanks in the telephone conversation below with the appropriate forms from the chart above.

LEYDIN: ¡Mamá, estoy aquí en los Estados Unidos!

MADRE: Hola, hija. ¿Cómo estás?

LEYDIN: Bien, mamá. Yo _____ muchas cosas ayer después de llegar.

MADRE: ¿Qué _____?

LEYDIN: Pues, primero les _____ los regalos a toda la familia.

MADRE: ¿Y la abuelita te _____ un regalo a ti, también?

LEYDIN: Sí, ¡una bicicleta nueva! Estoy muy contenta.

MADRE: Y, ¿qué _____ Uds. después?

LEYDIN: Los primos _____ la tarea y la abuelita y yo le _____ la lista

de cosas que comprar para la cena. Después le _____ la lista al abuelo,

quien _____ las compras en el supermercado.

MADRE: ¿_____ Uds. algo más?

LEYDIN: Sí. Después de comer, yo _____ un postre especial para todos: ¡tu

famoso pastel de tres leches!

MADRE: ¡Qué coincidencia! Yo _____ uno también y les _____ un

poco a nuestros amigos, los Sánchez. ¿Qué más . . .?

Go Online WEB CODE jcd-0814
PHSchool.com

Realidades

Capítulo 8B

Nombre _____

Fecha _____

Hora _____

Practice Workbook **8B–8**

Repaso

Across

2. Es importante ___ las latas de las calles.
4. Es necesario ayudar a los ___.
6. otra ___
10. *unforgettable*
13. el ___ de construcción

15.
16. lugar donde recogen las verduras y las plantas; el ___
20. AmeriCorps hace el trabajo ___.
22. Esa ___ es de cartón.
24. *problem*

Down

1. *poor*
3. Puedes reciclar una ___ de vidrio o de plástico.
5. *often*; __ ___
7. Puedes reciclar las botellas de ___ y de plástico.
8. Es importante reciclar las cajas de ___.
9. sinónimo de **las personas**; la ___
11. Los ___ son nuestro futuro.
12. el ___ de reciclaje

13.
14. El profesor ___ las botellas al centro de reciclaje.
17. el ___ Grande
18. *toy*; un ___
19. Mis padres me ___ la verdad.
21. sinónimo de **la comunidad**; el ___

23.

Realidades ①

Capítulo 8B

Nombre _____

Fecha _____

Hora _____

Practice Workbook **8B–9**

Organizer

I. Vocabulary

Places to do volunteer work

_____

_____

_____

_____

_____

Things that are recyclable

_____

_____

_____

_____

_____

Verbs to talk about recycling

_____

_____

_____

Words to describe experiences

_____

_____

_____

II. Grammar

1. The forms of **decir** in the present are: _____ _____

_____ _____

_____ _____

2. The indirect object pronouns are: _____ _____

_____ _____

_____ _____

3. The preterite forms of **dar** are: _____ _____

_____ _____

_____ _____

The preterite forms of **hacer** are: _____ _____

_____ _____

_____ _____

Go Online WEB CODE jcd-0817
PHSchool.com

Realidades ❶

Capítulo 9A

Nombre _____

Hora _____

Fecha _____

Practice Workbook **9A–1**

Las películas

A. You love movies, but always forget to check the newspaper for the showings. You constantly have to ask your friends what movies are showing and at what time. Complete each dialogue by filling in the words that best identify the picture.

1. —¿Cuándo empieza la _____?

   —Empieza a las nueve y media. Son casi las nueve. ¡Vamos ahora!

2. —¿Va a ser larga la _____?

   —Sí. Empieza a las dos y media y termina a las cinco menos cuarto.

3. —¿A qué hora dan la _____?

   —A las seis.

4. —¿Cuánto dura el _____?

   —Dura menos de tres horas.

5. —¿Cuándo va a empezar la _____?

   —Empieza a las cuatro y media.

6. —Ya es la una y veinte. ¿Qué podemos hacer?

   —Podemos ir al cine a ver una _____.

B. Now, say the following time expressions another way using new vocabulary phrases.

1. Son las cinco menos diez. _____.

2. Son las dos y treinta. _____.

3. Dura una hora y cincuenta minutos. Dura _____.

4. Termina a las once y cuarenta. Termina _____.

Realidades ①

Capítulo 9A

Nombre _____

Hora _____

Fecha _____

Practice Workbook **9A–2**

¿Qué programas les gustan?

Read the information about each person below. Then decide which TV program would be best for him or her and write it in the blank.

1. Pedro es gracioso. Siempre cuenta chistes y hace cosas cómicas. A él le gustan

   los programas _____.

2. Mi padre lee el periódico todos los días. Le interesa la política. A él le gustan

   los programas _____.

3. La profesora tiene dos hijos y quiere enseñarles mucho. También busca información

   para usar en la clase. Ella prefiere los programas _____.

4. Abuela no trabaja y tiene que estar en casa. Le interesan mucho los

   juegos, especialmente cuando la gente gana dinero. A ella le gustan los programas

   _____.

5. Javi toca la guitarra y Juanita canta. Pasan casi todo el tiempo practicando la

   música. A ellos les gustan los programas _____.

6. Rosa estudia inglés. Un día quiere trabajar para un periódico. Para aprender más

   de la gente, ella ve los programas _____.

7. Ronaldo es deportista. Juega al fútbol, al béisbol y al básquetbol. Cuando no está

   practicando un deporte está viendo programas _____.

8. A Cristina le gustan las historias. Lee novelas románticas y a veces escribe cuentos

   de amor. A ella le gustan las _____.

Go Online WEB CODE jcd-0901
PHSchool.com

Realidades ❶

Capítulo 9A

Nombre _____

Hora _____

Fecha _____

Practice Workbook 9A–3

¿Cómo son las cosas allí?

Luzma is writing a letter to her pen pal in the U.S. She is telling her pen pal about TV and movies in her country. Fill in the blanks with the words that best complete her thoughts.

Querida Valerie,

    ¿Qué tal? ¿Cómo fue la _____ que viste la semana pasada? En

mi país me encanta ir al cine. Me gustan más las películas _____.

Mi hermano es policía y _____ yo sé mucho _____

los policías. También me interesa esta clase de películas porque son más

_____ que una comedia o la ciencia ficción. Las comedias

_____ aburren y a veces son infantiles. No me gustan las películas

de _____ porque son demasiado violentas. ¿Qué _____

película te gusta más a ti?

    Ahora te hablo de los _____ de televisión aquí. Bueno, no son

muy diferentes de los programas de allí. Tenemos programas de dibujos

animados como Rin, ran, run, programas de _____ como ¡Una

fortuna para ti! y tenemos las noticias. Yo veo las noticias pero sólo me

interesan los programas que dan sobre la policía en el _____ 56.

    Eso es todo. Adiós, amiga.

                          Luzma

Realidades ➊

Capítulo 9A

Nombre _____

Hora _____

Fecha _____

Practice Workbook **9A–4**

Tus programas favoritos

Read the TV listings below, then answer the questions that follow in complete sentences.

EVENING — NOCHE		8PM

EVENING — NOCHE

6PM
- **2** Noticias
- **18** Amigos
- **26** Noticias
- **30** Pepito y Paquito
- **33** Mi casa
- **42** Deportivas
- **60** Música cubana

7pm
- **2** Los monos
- **18** Noticias
- **26** Entre tú y yo
- **30** Noticias
- **33** Noticias
- **42** Deportes
- **60** La salsa y la samba

8PM
- **2** ¡Niágara!
- **18** Amigos
- **26** Película: El monstruo verde
- **30** El mundo real
- **33** Hoy día
- **42** Fútbol . . . .
- **60** ¿Puedes cantar?

9PM
- **2** El zoológico
- **18** Mi Amiga Sara
- **26** . . . .
- **30** El día en Alaska
- **33** ¡Ganar un coche!
- **42** . . . .
- **60** Baile en vivo

1. ¿Cuántos programas de noticias empiezan a las seis? _____

2. ¿Qué clase de programas tiene el canal 42? _____

   ¿Y el canal 60? _____

   ¿Y el canal 2? _____

3. ¿Qué programa deportivo puedes ver a las ocho? _____

   _____

4. Para ver un programa educativo, ¿vas a ver el canal 2 o el 18 a las nueve? _____

   _____

5. ¿Qué clase de programa empieza a las nueve en el canal 33? _____

   ¿Y a las nueve en el canal 30? _____

6. ¿Qué clase de programa dan a las siete en el canal 26? _____

7. ¿Dan una película de horror a las ocho en el canal 26?

   _____

Go Online WEB CODE jcd-0902
PHSchool.com

Acabo de . . .

Write what the following people just finished doing and are now going to do, based on the pictures. Follow the model.

Modelo   Marta *acaba de estudiar. Ahora va a dormir.*

1. Anabel _____

_____

2. Nosotros _____

_____

3. Ellas _____

_____

4. Yo _____

_____

5. Tú _____

_____

6. Juan y el Sr. Lebredo _____

_____

7. Roberto _____

_____

8. Ana María _____

_____

Más gustos

A. Complete the sentences below with the correct forms of the verbs given.

1. Al Presidente le _____ (interesar) la política.

2. ¡Qué terrible! Me _____ (doler) el pie izquierdo.

3. A los estudiantes les _____ (aburrir) las presentaciones largas.

4. A nosotros nos _____ (encantar) ver comedias.

5. A tus hermanos les _____ (gustar) las películas de horror.

6. A ti te _____ (interesar) el teatro.

7. Me _____ (quedar) bien los pantalones pero me

   _____ (faltar) el dinero para comprarlos.

B. Now, complete each sentence below with the correct form of the verb given and the appropriate indirect object pronoun. Follow the model.

Modelo   A Carlos _____*le aburre*_____ (aburrir) la política.

1. A mí _____ (faltar) un lápiz.

2. A ellas _____ (aburrir) las clases de arte.

3. A Carmen _____ (quedar) bien la falda, ¿no?

4. A ti _____ (encantar) los programas deportivos.

5. ¿A ti y a Pedro _____ (gustar) leer revistas?

6. A mi papá _____ (doler) los pies.

7. ¿A Ud. _____ (faltar) los cuadernos?

8. A nosotros _____ (interesar) las obras de teatro.

9. A Lola y a Roberto _____ (interesar) el programa musical y el programa educativo.

Realidades ①

Capítulo 9A

Nombre _____

Hora _____

Fecha _____

Practice Workbook **9A–7**

Frases revueltas

The following sentences are mixed up. Rearrange them so that they are grammatically correct and make sense. Don't forget to conjugate verbs where appropriate. Follow the model.

Modelo ir al cine / me / a mí / y al centro comercial / gustar

A mí me gusta ir al cine y al centro comercial.

1. le / leer / a Elena / poemas / encantar / y escribir

   _____

2. negros / unos zapatos / te / para / faltar / a ti / ir a la fiesta

   _____

3. diez kilómetros / a mí / doler / después de / me / los pies / correr

   _____

4. al Sr. Mirabal / interesar / americano / le / el fútbol

   _____

5. los programas / les / a mis padres / de entrevistas / aburrir

   _____

6. importar / voluntario / a nosotros / el trabajo / nos

   _____

7. a Uds. / los boletos para el cine / les / para comprar / faltar / el dinero

   _____

8. interesar / les / a José y a Felipe / policíacas / las películas

   _____

9. el trabajo / a Angélica / aburrir / le

   _____

10. la comida / italiana / encantar / a Vanessa y a mí / nos

    _____

Realidades **1**

Capítulo 9A

Nombre _____

Hora _____

Fecha _____

Practice Workbook **9A–8**

Repaso

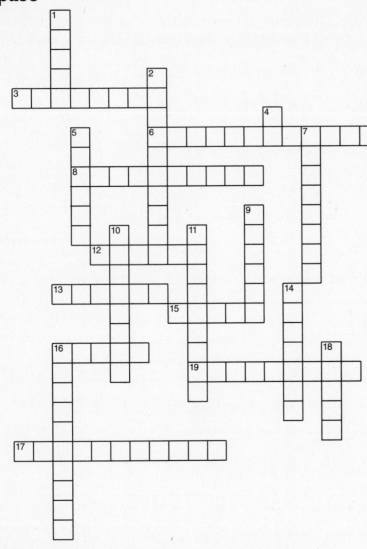

Down

1. Yo veo mis programas favoritos en el ____ cinco.
2. Es más que interesante; es ____.
4. *already*
5. No es actor, es ____.
7. No es interesante, es ____.
9. Me van a ____ zapatos. Necesito comprarlos.
10. Puedes leer las ____ o verlas en la tele.

11. película ____
14. *really?*
16. A Paco le gusta el fútbol. Ve programas ____.
18. No sé mucho ____ eso.

Across

3. Cuando vas al cine, ves una ____.

6.
8. un programa en la tele que cuenta las historias románticas de la gente; la ____
12. *therefore*
13. Una comedia es ____.
15. No es actriz, es ____.
16. Los programas ____ una hora.
17. ***Entre tú y yo*** es un programa de ____.
19. Cuando la gente gana dinero, es un programa de ____.

Realidades 1

Capítulo 9A

Nombre _____

Fecha _____

Hora _____

Practice Workbook **9A–9**

Organizer

I. Vocabulary

Types of television programs

_____
_____
_____
_____
_____
_____
_____

Types of movies

_____
_____
_____
_____
_____
_____
_____

Words to describe movies/programs

_____
_____
_____
_____
_____

Words to express opinions

_____
_____
_____
_____
_____

II. Grammar

1. Use _____ + _____ to say what you or others have just finished doing.

2. **Me gusta** is literally translated as "_____". So, the construction is formed by putting the _____ first, followed by the _____, and finally the _____.

Realidades 1

Capítulo 9B

Nombre _____

Fecha _____

Hora _____

Practice Workbook **9B–1**

El laboratorio

Label the computer lab below with the appropriate words.

1. _____   4. _____

2. _____   5. _____

3. _____   6. _____

Las asociaciones

Write the words from your vocabulary that you associate with each of the following definitions.

1. Una sala de clases con muchas computadoras   _____

2. Lugar para hablar con otras personas en línea   _____

3. Comunicarse con otros por computadora   _____

4. Lo que haces si quieres aprender más   _____

5. Buscar información   _____

6. Un lugar de la Red dedicado a algún tema   _____

7. Hacer actividades electrónicas divertidas   _____

8. Una comunicación *no* por correo electrónico   _____

9. Una carta que envías para una fecha especial   _____

10. Expresar y comprender ideas de otra persona   _____

11. Si quieres hacer un disco compacto   _____

12. Un artista puede hacerlos en la computadora   _____

Realidades 1

Capítulo 9B

Nombre _____

Hora _____

Fecha _____

Practice Workbook **9B–3**

El sitio Web

Sara has just purchased a laptop computer. She is so excited that she just has to tell her friend Ramón. In the e-mail below write the words that best complete her thoughts.

Ramón,

    Ay, amigo, tienes que comprarte una computadora

_____. ¡Son los mejores juguetes del mundo!

Cuando vas de vacaciones puedes llevarla en tu mochila y

cuando estás en el hotel puedes _____ en la

Red, escribir por _____ o

_____ información de la Red. ¿Y quieres

sacar fotos? Con una cámara _____ puedes

sacarlas y ponerlas en la computadora. También puedes

mandar las fotos a otra _____ electrónica

si quieres. ¿Qué te _____? ¿Es difícil?

Puedes _____ un curso para aprender más

sobre cómo usar esta clase de cámara y cómo crear

_____ en la computadora. No debes tener

_____ de buscar información sobre

cámaras digitales porque hay muchas personas que

_____ usarlas o que escribieron unos

_____ sobre estas cámaras.

    Bueno, podemos hablar más de esto _____

porque no tengo tiempo ahora. Hasta luego.

Sara

Realidades **1**

Capítulo 9B

Nombre _____

Fecha _____

Hora _____

Practice Workbook **9B–4**

¡Una computadora muy buena!

Your local newspaper recently ran an ad for a new computer and many of your friends bought one. Read some of the computer's capabilities in the ad below. Then, based on the information you are given about each person that bought this computer, say what he or she uses the new computer for. Follow the model.

CON LA COMPUTADORA ES POSIBLE:

- Grabar un disco compacto
- Preparar presentaciones
- Escribir por correo electrónico
- Usar una cámara digital
- Visitar salones de chat
- Navegar en la Red
- Crear documentos
- Estar en línea

Modelo   A Juan le gusta bajar información.

Juan usa la computadora para estar en línea.

1. A Alejandro le gusta escribir cuentos y composiciones.

_____

2. A Diego le gusta sacar fotos.

_____

3. A Caridad le gusta tocar y escuchar música.

_____

4. A Ramiro le gusta buscar los sitios Web.

_____

5. A Esperanza le gusta conocer y hablar con otras personas.

_____

6. A Lucita le gusta escribir tarjetas y cartas a su familia que vive en otra ciudad.

_____

7. A Rodrigo le gusta enseñar a los niños.

_____

Realidades ❶

Capítulo 9B

Nombre _____

Fecha _____

Hora _____

Practice Workbook **9B–5**

¿Pedir o servir?

A. Fill in the charts below with the present tense forms of the verbs **pedir** and **servir**.

	PEDIR	SERVIR
yo	pido	
tú		
él, ella, Ud.		sirve
nosotros		
vosotros	pedís	servís
ellos, ellas, Uds.		

B. Complete the mini-conversations below with the correct forms of **pedir** or **servir**.

1. —Cuando vas al restaurante Marino para comer, ¿qué _____ tú?

   —Normalmente _____ una ensalada y una pasta.

2. —¿Para qué _____ esto?

   —_____ para grabar discos compactos, hijo.

3. —¿Los camareros les _____ rápidamente en el restaurante Guzmán?

   —Sí, son muy trabajadores.

4. —No puedo ver esos gráficos.

   —(Nosotros) _____ ayuda, entonces.

5. —Bienvenida a la fiesta. ¿Le _____ algo?

   —Sí, un refresco, por favor.

6. —Vamos al restaurante. Esta noche ellos _____ pollo con salsa y pasta.

   —Yo siempre _____ el pollo.

7. —¿Para qué _____ el menú?

   —_____ para conocer la comida del restaurante. ¿Y qué vas a

   _____ del menú?

   —Yo siempre _____ la misma cosa. . . el bistec.

Go Online WEB CODE jcd-0913
PHSchool.com

Realidades 1

Capítulo 9B

Nombre _____

Hora _____

Fecha _____

Practice Workbook **9B–6**

¿Saber o conocer?

A. Write either **saber** or **conocer** in the blanks under the items below.

1. Mi número de teléfono

_____

2. Usar una computadora

_____

3. El profesor de la clase de español

_____

4. La película *Casablanca*

_____

5. Leer música

_____

6. La ciudad de Nueva York

_____

7. Mi madre

_____

8. Tu mejor amigo

_____

9. Navegar en la Red

_____

10. El sitio Web

_____

B. Fill in the missing forms of **saber** and **conocer** in the charts below.

	SABER	CONOCER
yo		
tú		
él, ella, Ud.	*sabe*	*conoce*
nosotros		
vosotros	*sabéis*	*conocéis*
ellos, ellas, Uds.		

C. Complete the following sentences using the correct forms of **saber** or **conocer**.

1. Juan, ¿ _____ la fecha de hoy?

2. ¿Alguien _____ a un médico bueno?

3. Mis padres _____ bailar muy bien.

4. Nosotros _____ todas las palabras de la obra.

5. ¿_____ dónde está el Museo del Prado?

WEB CODE jcd-0914
PHSchool.com

Manos a la obra — *Gramática* **171**

Realidades ①

Capítulo 9B

Nombre _____

Hora _____

Fecha _____

Practice Workbook **9B–7**

Planes para la noche

The Miranda family is planning to go out to eat. Fill in their conversation using forms of **conocer, saber, pedir,** or **servir**.

PADRE: Vamos al restaurante Vista del Mar. ¿Lo _____ Uds.? Me gusta

mucho.

TERESA: Yo no lo _____ pero _____ dónde está. ¡Quiero ir

a ese restaurante!

TOMÁS: Por supuesto que _____ dónde está, Tere, el nombre es Vista del Mar.

TERESA: Sí. ¿_____ Uds. que tienen el mejor pescado de la ciudad?

Es muy sabroso.

MADRE: ¿Y ellos _____ otra comida también?

TERESA: Yo no _____ . ¿Sabes tú, Tomás?

TOMÁS: Sí. Allí _____ mucha comida rica.

PADRE: Yo _____ el pescado porque me encanta.

TOMÁS: Sí, me encanta el pescado también.

TERESA: Es verdad Tomás, pero siempre _____ la misma cosa cuando

comemos pescado.

PADRE: Por eso vamos a este restaurante. Puedes _____ de todo y va a ser

sabrosísimo.

TERESA: ¡Yo quiero _____ ese restaurante!

MADRE: Pues, estamos de acuerdo. Vamos a Vista del Mar.

Go Online WEB CODE jcd-0915
PHSchool.com

Realidades ①

Capítulo 9B

Nombre _____

Hora _____

Fecha _____

Practice Workbook **9B–8**

Repaso

Down

1.

2. El cliente ___ un té helado porque tiene calor.

3. Voy a visitar Nueva York porque quiero ___ la.

4. ___ un disco compacto

6. Los estudiantes hacen un ___ del presidente Lincoln.

8. Quiero escribirte una carta. ¿Cuál es tu ___ electrónica?

9. Yo escribo por ___ electrónico.

11. Estoy en línea. Quiero ___ en __ ___.

12. *song*; la ___

13. El ___ Web para este libro es *PHSchool.com*.

14. No tengo ese programa. Lo voy a ___ de la Red.

16. Necesito ___ información para mi informe.

18. La artista sabe muy bien hacer ___ en la computadora.

19. Necesito una computadora que puede ___ documentos.

21. *slide*; la ___

Across

1. Quiero ___ un curso.

5. No debes tener ___ de la tecnología.

7. Para navegar en la Red, hay que estar ___ ___.

10. Si quieres hablar con personas inmediatamente, vas a un ___ de chat.

13. ¿Para qué ___?

15. *to communicate (with)*

17. Mi amiga me escribió una ___.

20. No me gusta hablar por teléfono. Me gusta hablar ___ __ __.

22. Voy a la escuela porque quiero ___ cómo hacer cosas.

23. Vamos al ___ para usar las computadoras de la escuela.

24. la computadora ___

Organizer

I. Vocabulary

Words to talk about the Web

_____

_____

_____

_____

Words to name other electronics

_____

_____

_____

_____

Verbs related to online activities

_____

_____

_____

_____

_____

II. Grammar

1. The present tense of **pedir** is: The present tense of **servir** is:

_____ _____   _____ _____

_____ _____   _____ _____

_____ _____   _____ _____

2. Use the verb _____ for information or activities that you know. Use

   the verb _____ to talk about familiarity with people, places, or things.

Writing, Audio & Video Activities

Actividad 1

You are at a party with students visiting from Ecuador. You have practiced several responses to the things they might say when you meet them. Listen to each question or statement and write the letter of the best response in the blank. You will hear each statement or question twice.

a. Me llamo ...   **1.** _____

b. Muy bien, gracias. **2.** _____

c. Regular.   **3.** _____

d. Mucho gusto.   **4.** _____

e. Igualmente.   **5.** _____

f. Hasta mañana.   **6.** _____

Actividad 2

You have lost your dog, so you put up signs in your neighborhood asking your neighbors to call you if they see him. You will hear six messages on your answering machine from neighbors who have seen your dog. You will not understand everything they say, but listen carefully to find out their house number and what time they called so that you can track down your dog. Write down each house number and time on the chart. You will hear each message twice.

	NÚMERO DE CASA (House number)	HORA DE LA LLAMADA (Time of call)
1.	_____	_____
2.	_____	_____
3.	_____	_____
4.	_____	_____
5.	_____	_____
6.	_____	_____

Realidades 1

Nombre _____

Hora _____

Para empezar

Fecha _____

AUDIO

Actividad 3

A new student has come into your Spanish class. He seems lost when the teacher asks the students to take out certain items. As you listen to what the teacher says, help him by identifying the picture that matches the item the teacher is asking the students to get out for class. You will hear each command twice.

Modelo ____f____ 1. _____ 2. _____ 3. _____ 4. _____ 5. _____

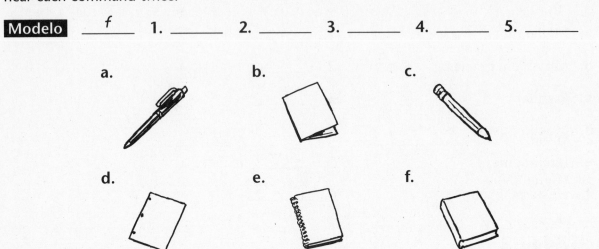

a.

b.

c.

d.

e.

f.

Actividad 4

Your teacher is using a map and an alphabet/number grid to plan a class trip to Spain. The five dots on the grid represent cities in Spain where your group will stop. Listen as you hear the first letter/number combination, as in the game of Bingo. Find that dot on the grid and label it "1." Next to it, write the name of the city. After you hear the second letter/number combination, find the second dot and label it "2," writing the name of the city next to it, and so on for the rest of the dots. Connect the dots to show the route of the class trip. You will hear each phrase twice.

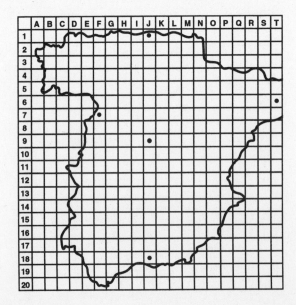

Actividad 5

While on vacation in Uruguay, your teacher visits an elementary school classroom. Each student in the class tells your teacher his or her birthday (**cumpleaños**) and what the weather is like at that time of the year in Uruguay. Remember, in South America the seasons are the reverse of those in the United States. In the first column write out each student's date of birth, and in the second column what season his or her birthday is in. You will hear each sentence twice.

	DATE OF BIRTH	SEASON
1. Juan	_____	_____
2. María	_____	_____
3. Miguel	_____	_____
4. Óscar	_____	_____
5. Carolina	_____	_____
6. Marta	_____	_____
7. Elena	_____	_____
8. Pedro	_____	_____

Realidades ❶

Nombre _____

Hora _____

Para empezar

Fecha _____

WRITING

Actividad 6

Describe the monster below, telling how many of each body part he has (**El monstruo tiene ...**). Each blank corresponds to one letter. Each letter corresponds to a number, which appears underneath the blank. Use these numbers to figure out which sentence refers to which body part. The first one has been done for you.

Modelo   El monstruo tiene $\underset{9}{D}\ \underset{15}{O}\ \underset{20}{S}$ $\underset{2}{C}\ \underset{10}{A}\ \underset{19}{B}\ \underset{1}{E}\ \underset{3}{Z}\ \underset{10}{A}\ \underset{20}{S}$.

1. El monstruo tiene $\underset{15}{\ }\ \underset{2}{\ }\ \underset{8}{\ }\ \underset{15}{\ }$ $\underset{15}{\ }\ \underset{17}{\ }\ \underset{15}{\ }\ \underset{20}{\ }$.

2. El monstruo tiene $\underset{6}{\ }\ \underset{22}{\ }\ \underset{10}{\ }$ $\underset{22}{\ }\ \underset{10}{\ }\ \underset{4}{\ }\ \underset{5}{\ }\ \underset{3}{\ }$ en cada cabeza.

3. El monstruo tiene $\underset{6}{\ }\ \underset{22}{\ }\ \underset{10}{\ }$ $\underset{19}{\ }\ \underset{15}{\ }\ \underset{2}{\ }\ \underset{10}{\ }$ en cada cabeza.

4. El monstruo tiene $\underset{2}{\ }\ \underset{6}{\ }\ \underset{10}{\ }\ \underset{11}{\ }\ \underset{4}{\ }\ \underset{15}{\ }$ $\underset{19}{\ }\ \underset{4}{\ }\ \underset{10}{\ }\ \underset{3}{\ }\ \underset{15}{\ }\ \underset{20}{\ }$.

5. El monstruo tiene $\underset{11}{\ }\ \underset{4}{\ }\ \underset{1}{\ }\ \underset{20}{\ }$ $\underset{9}{\ }\ \underset{1}{\ }\ \underset{9}{\ }\ \underset{15}{\ }\ \underset{20}{\ }$ en cada mano.

6. El monstruo tiene $\underset{20}{\ }\ \underset{1}{\ }\ \underset{5}{\ }\ \underset{20}{\ }$ $\underset{16}{\ }\ \underset{5}{\ }\ \underset{1}{\ }\ \underset{4}{\ }\ \underset{22}{\ }\ \underset{10}{\ }\ \underset{20}{\ }$.

Actividad 7

A. It is September and school is finally in session. You already have some important dates to mark on the calendar. To make sure you have the right day, write the day of the week that each date falls on.

SEPTIEMBRE						
lunes	martes	miércoles	jueves	viernes	sábado	domingo
		1	2	3	4	5
6	7	8	9	10	11	12
13	14	15	16	17	18	19
20	21	22	23	24	25	26
27	28	29	30			

1. el tres de septiembre _____

2. el veinte de septiembre _____

3. el primero de septiembre _____

4. el veinticuatro de septiembre _____

5. el doce de septiembre _____

6. el dieciocho de septiembre _____

7. el siete de septiembre _____

B. Now, write in what month the following holidays occur.

1. el Día de San Valentín _____

2. el Día de San Patricio _____

3. la Navidad _____

4. el Año Nuevo _____

5. el Día de la Independencia _____

Realidades ❶

Para empezar

Nombre _____

Fecha _____

Hora _____

WRITING

Actividad 8

Answer the questions below according to the map.

1. ¿Qué tiempo hace en el norte de México?

    _____

2. ¿Hace buen tiempo en el sur?

    _____

3. ¿Qué tiempo hace en el centro de México?

    _____

4. ¿Hace frío o calor en el oeste?

    _____

5. ¿Qué tiempo hace en el este?

    _____

6. ¿Qué estación es, probablemente?

    _____

Nombre _____ Hora _____

Fecha _____

Introducción

Actividad 1

Do you like the video so far? Did you enjoy meeting the characters? Are you curious to find out more about their home cities? Look at the map below. Then, write the names of the video friends that live at each location. As you are doing this exercise, begin to familiarize yourself with the names of these locations: Madrid, España; Ciudad de México, México; San José, Costa Rica; San Antonio, Texas.

Esteban y Angélica	Ignacio y Ana	Claudia y Teresa	Raúl y Gloria

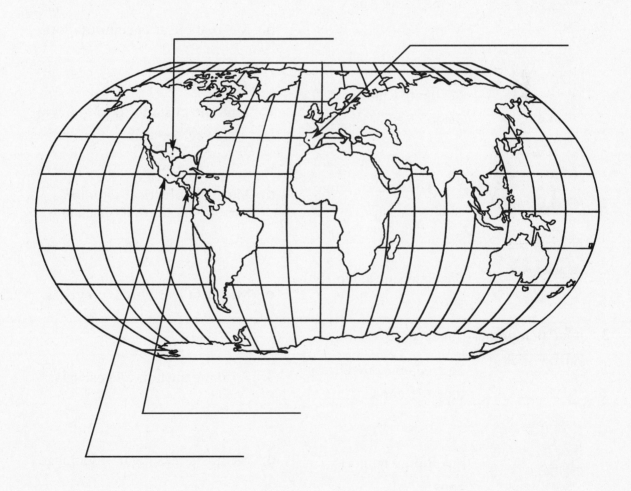

¿Comprendes?

Actividad 2

Match the characters with the activities they like to do or do not like to do.

1. Me llamo Ignacio y tengo 17 años. _____

     a. Me gusta escuchar música también. Pero me gusta más hablar por teléfono.

2. Yo me llamo Ana y tengo 15 años. _____

     b. Me gusta usar la computadora.

3. Me llamo Claudia y tengo 16 años. _____

     c. A mí me gusta tocar la guitarra.

4. Y yo soy Teresa. Tengo 15 años. _____

     d. Me gusta practicar deportes, correr y montar en bicicleta.

5. Soy Esteban. Tengo 15 años. _____

     e. Me gusta leer libros y revistas.

6. Yo me llamo Angélica y tengo 16 años. _____

     f. A mí me gusta ir a la escuela.

7. Soy Raúl y tengo 15 años. _____

     g. Me gusta más jugar videojuegos.

8. Me llamo Gloria y tengo 14 años. _____

     h. A mí no me gusta ni correr ni montar en bicicleta. A mí me gusta patinar.

Actividad 3

Decide whether response a, b, or c best describes the characters in each question.

1. When they are outside, what does Ana ask Ignacio? _____
   a. ¿Te gusta hablar por teléfono?
   b. ¿Qué te gusta hacer?
   c. ¿Te gusta tocar la guitarra?

2. Claudia and Teresa live in Mexico. What do they both like to do? _____
   a. pasar tiempo con amigos
   b. jugar videojuegos
   c. usar la computadora

3. What sports do Esteban and Angélica talk about? _____
   a. correr, montar en bicicleta y patinar
   b. esquiar, correr y nadar
   c. jugar al básquetbol, jugar al fútbol y montar en bicicleta

4. Does Raúl like to go to school? _____
   a. Sí. A Raúl le gusta mucho ir a la escuela.
   b. No. No le gusta nada.
   c. Pues… más o menos.

Y, ¿qué más?

Actividad 4

You have just seen and heard what these eight video friends like or do not like to do. Now fill in the blanks below to tell about things that you like to do and do not like to do.

1. Me gusta _____.

2. A mí me gusta más _____.

3. A mí no me gusta _____.

4. A mí no me gusta ni _____.

Realidades

Capítulo 1A

Nombre _____

Fecha _____

Hora _____

AUDIO

Actividad 5

You can learn a lot about a person from what he or she likes to do. You will hear two people from each group of three describe themselves. Listen and match the descriptions to the appropriate pictures. Put an *A* underneath the first person described, and a *B* underneath the second person described. You will hear each set of statements twice.

1. Luisa _____ Marta _____ Carmen _____

2. Marco _____ Javier _____ Alejandro _____

3. Mercedes _____ Ana _____ María _____

4. Carlos _____ Jaime _____ Luis _____

5. Isabel _____ Margarita _____ Cristina _____

Actividad 6

A group of students from Peru will visit your school. Since your class will be hosting the students, your teacher is trying to match each of you with a visiting student who likes to do the same things as you do. Listen to the questions and write the students' answers in the blanks. Then, write which of the activities you like better. Find out if the student has the same preferences as you do. Follow the model. You will hear each conversation twice.

Modelo   Guillermo: _____*cantar*_____

A mí: ____*Me gusta más bailar*____ .

1. Paco: _____

   A mí: _____ .

2. Ana María: _____

   A mí: _____ .

3. José Luis: _____

   A mí: _____ .

4. Maricarmen: _____

   A mí: _____ .

5. Luisa: _____

   A mí: _____ .

Actividad 7

As one of the judges at your school's fall carnival, your job is to mark on the master tic tac toe board the progress of a live tic-tac-toe competition between Team X and Team O.

As each contestant comes to the microphone, you will hear "por X" or "por O" to indicate for which team he or she is playing. The contestant has to answer a question about activities in order to claim the square. Listen for the activity mentioned in each question, and put either an *X* or an *O* in the box under the picture of that activity.

At the end of this game round, see which team won! You will hear each statement twice.

Who won the game? _____

Realidades ❶

Capítulo 1A

Nombre _____

Fecha _____

Hora _____

AUDIO

Actividad 8

Luisa, the host of your school's radio station talk show, is interviewing four new students. As you listen to the interview, write down one thing that each student likes to do, and one thing that each student does not like to do. You will hear the entire question and answer session repeated. You will hear this conversation twice.

	Armando	**Josefina**	**Carlos**	**Marta**
Likes				
Dislikes				

Actividad 9

As you turn on the radio, you hear a Spanish radio D.J. talking about the "Top Ten Tips" for being happy during this school year. As you listen, match the suggestion to one of the pictures and number them in the order the suggestions were given on the air. Remember to listen for cognates!

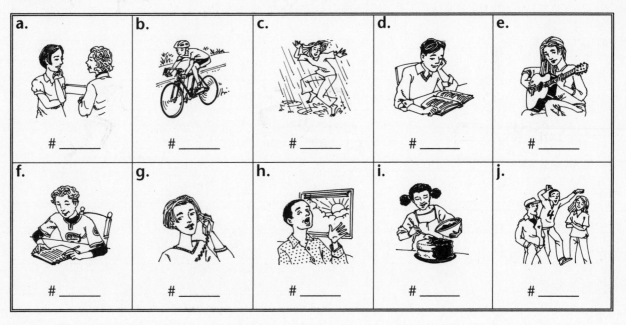

a. # _____   b. # _____   c. # _____   d. # _____   e. # _____

f. # _____   g. # _____   h. # _____   i. # _____   j. # _____

Actividad 10

Students like to do all sorts of activities during their free periods. Look at the picture below and write what each student is saying he or she likes to do. Then say whether or not you like to do those things. Follow the model.

| Modelo | EL PROFESOR: | *A mí me gusta trabajar.* |

TÚ: *A mí me gusta trabajar también.*

ESTUDIANTE #1: _____

TÚ: _____

ESTUDIANTE #2: _____

TÚ: _____

ESTUDIANTE #3: _____

TÚ: _____

ESTUDIANTE #4: _____

TÚ: _____

ESTUDIANTE #5: _____

TÚ: _____

ESTUDIANTE #6: _____

TÚ: _____

Actividad 11

It is your first day at your new school, and your new friend Elena is interviewing you for the school newspaper. In the spaces provided, write your answers to the questions that Elena asks you.

ELENA: —Buenos días. ¿Cómo estás?

TÚ: —_____

ELENA: —¿Qué te gusta hacer?

TÚ: —_____

ELENA: —¿Te gusta ir a la escuela?

TÚ: —_____

ELENA: —¿Qué te gusta hacer en casa?

TÚ: —_____

ELENA: —¿Te gusta escribir o leer cuentos?

TÚ: —_____

ELENA: —¿Qué más te gusta hacer?

TÚ: —_____

ELENA: —Pues, muchas gracias por la entrevista. Buena suerte.

TÚ: —_____

Realidades 1

Capítulo 1A

Nombre _____

Fecha _____

Hora _____

WRITING

Actividad 12

A. Your classmates have signed up for different clubs. Look at the flyers below to see who signed up for which club. Then, decide how each student might answer the questions below based on the club that each one signed up for.

El Club Educativo	El Club Deportista	EL CLUB MUSICAL
El club ideal para estudiantes a quienes les gusta ir a la escuela.	El club ideal para estudiantes a quienes les gusta practicar deportes.	El club ideal para estudiantes a quienes les gusta la música.
Actividades:	Actividades:	**ACTIVIDADES:**
• usar la computadora • leer y escribir cuentos • estudiar	• nadar • correr • practicar deportes	• TOCAR EL PIANO O LA GUITARRA • CANTAR • BAILAR
Eduardo _____ Eugenia _____ Esteban _____	Diana _____ Dolores _____ Diego _____	MARICARMEN _____ MANOLO _____ MÓNICA _____

Modelo Eduardo, ¿te gusta tocar la guitarra?

No, no me gusta tocar la guitarra. Me gusta estudiar.

1. Diana, ¿te gusta leer o escribir cuentos?

_____

2. Manolo, ¿qué te gusta hacer?

_____

3. Diego, ¿te gusta ir a la escuela para usar la computadora?

_____

4. Mónica, ¿te gusta nadar o correr?

_____

5. Eugenia, ¿qué te gusta hacer?

_____

B. Now, pick which club you would join and say why. Follow the model.

Modelo *Prefiero el Club Educativo porque me gusta ir a la escuela.*

Prefiero el Club _____ porque _____

_____

Actividad 13

A. Write two sentences about things that you like to do, and two sentences about things that you do not like to do. Follow the model.

Modelo *A mí me gusta leer.*

  No me gusta correr.

1. _____

2. _____

3. _____

4. _____

B. Now, use your sentences from Part A to write a letter to your new penpal that will tell her a little bit about you.

29/9/2003

Saludos,

_____

_____

_____

_____

_____

También _____

_____

_____

_____

Un abrazo,

_____

Realidades ①

Capítulo 1B

Nombre _____

Hora _____

Fecha _____

VIDEO

Antes de ver el video

Actividad 1

During the video, Teresa, Claudia, Pedro, and Esteban describe each other in e-mails. How would you describe yourself? Below is a list of descriptive words. Check off the words that describe you.

Soy... ❏ artístico, -a   ❏ impaciente   ❏ simpático, -a

❏ atrevido, -a   ❏ inteligente   ❏ sociable

❏ deportista   ❏ ordenado, -a   ❏ talentoso, -a

❏ desordenado, -a   ❏ paciente   ❏ trabajador, -ora

❏ estudioso, -a   ❏ reservado, -a

❏ gracioso, -a   ❏ serio, -a

¿Comprendes?

Actividad 2

Fill in the blanks with the appropriate word or phrase from the bank. You may have to watch the video several times to remember each character well.

misteriosa	reservado	ordenados	inteligente
serio	trabajadora	sociable	
simpática	hablar por teléfono	buena	

1.  A Pedro no le gusta ni bailar ni cantar. Es _____.

Pero él escribe: "Soy muy gracioso. No soy muy _____."

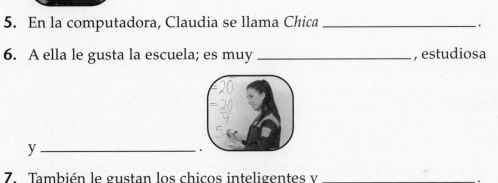

2. Teresa, desde un cibercafé en la Ciudad de México, escribe: "Yo soy *Chica*

_____ ."

3. Ella es la _____ amiga de Claudia.

4. Le gusta _____ , pero no le gusta ir a la escuela.

5. En la computadora, Claudia se llama *Chica* _____ .

6. A ella le gusta la escuela; es muy _____ , estudiosa

y _____ .

7. También le gustan los chicos inteligentes y _____ .

8. A Pedro le gusta *Chica misteriosa*. Ella también es una chica _____

Actividad 3

According to Esteban, Pedro is quiet and reserved. Yet, in his e-mail, he writes the opposite. Read what he writes about himself in his e-mail. Then, write what he is really like by filling in the blanks.

> Me llamo Chico sociable. ¡Qué coincidencia! Me gusta pasar tiempo con mis amigos... Me gusta escuchar música. Según mis amigos soy muy gracioso. No soy muy serio.   Escríbeme.

1. *Chico sociable*, el _____ de Esteban, se llama _____ .

2. Según Esteban, él no es un chico _____ . Él es _____ .

3. A Pedro no le gusta ni _____ ni _____ .

4. Pedro no es muy _____ . Él es muy _____ .

Y, ¿qué más?

Actividad 4

Describe people you know using each of the adjectives from the following list. Follow the model.

paciente	inteligente	sociable	impaciente	deportista

Modelo   *La profesora de español es muy inteligente.*

_____

_____

_____

_____

Actividad 5

You are a volunteer for a service at your school that helps new students meet other new students in order to make the transition easier. People who are interested in participating in this program have left messages describing themselves. Listen as the students describe themselves, and put a check mark in at least two columns that match what each student says. Then write the names of the most well-matched students. You will hear each statement twice.

BUENOS AMIGOS

	CARMEN	PABLO	ANA	ANDRÉS	RAQUEL	JORGE
serio(a)						
reservado(a)						
deportista						
estudioso(a)						
talentoso(a)						
gracioso(a)						
atrevido(a)						
trabajador(a)						
artístico(a)						
sociable						
romántico(a)						

BUENOS AMIGOS:

1. _____ y _____

2. _____ y _____

3. _____ y _____

Realidades ❶

Capítulo 1B

Nombre _____

Hora _____

Fecha _____

AUDIO

Actividad 6

What is your favorite season of the year? Your choice could say a lot about you. Listen as talk-show psychologist Doctor Armando describes people according to their preferred season (**estación preferida**) of the year. What characteristics go with each season? Listen and put a check mark in the appropriate boxes. By the way, is it true what he says about you and your favorite season? You will hear each statement twice.

Mi estación preferida es _____. Según el Dr. Armando, yo soy

_____.

Realidades ❶

Capítulo 1B

Nombre _____

Hora _____

Fecha _____

AUDIO

Actividad 7

Your Spanish teacher encourages you to speak Spanish outside of class. As you walk down the hall, you hear parts of your classmates' conversations in Spanish. Listen to the conversations and decide whether they are talking about a boy, a girl, or if you can't tell by what is being said. Place a check mark in the appropriate box of the table. You will hear each statement twice.

	#1	#2	#3	#4	#5	#6	#7	#8
🧍								
🧍‍♀️								
?								

Actividad 8

Listen as Nacho describes his ex-girlfriend. How many things do they have in common? Put an X on the pictures that show ways in which they are very different and put a circle around the pictures that show ways they are very similar. You will hear each set of statements twice.

1.

2.

3.

4.

5.

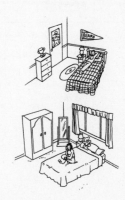

Realidades ❶

Capítulo 1B

Nombre _____

Fecha _____

Hora _____

AUDIO

Actividad 9

Some people say we are what we dream! Listen as Antonieta calls in and describes her dream (**sueño**) to Doctor Armando, the radio talk show psychologist. Draw a circle around the pictures below that match what she dreams about herself.

After you hear Antonieta's call, tell a partner what kinds of things would be in a dream that reveals what you like to do and what kind of person you are. You might begin with "**En mi sueño, me gusta...**". You will hear this dialogue twice.

Actividad 10

A. Fill in the words using the art as clues.

1. Marta es una chica _____.

2. Cristina es mi amiga _____.

3. Alicia es muy _____.

4. Isa es una chica _____.

5. Alejandro es muy _____.

6. Carlos es un chico _____.

7. Kiko es _____.

8. Pepe es mi amigo _____.

B. Now, check your answers by finding them in the word search.

```
N E P M V P I Q U U T D
T R A B A J A D O R A E
A S O I D U T S E D G S
L A K U X M A L E A R O
E M D I C Z P P O C A R
N T P A O X O J Z I C D
T I U M N R U F R T I E
O Q K I T E I T E S O N
S M X I E T D G P I S A
A O S L U R M R Y T O D
P T L A E U U J O R H O
A S O C I A B L E A E T
```

Realidades ①

Capítulo 1B

Nombre _____

Fecha _____

Hora _____

WRITING

Actividad 11

Frida and Diego, who are opposites, are talking on the phone. Frida, the sociable one, is doing all the talking. Using the pictures of the friends below, write what Frida might be saying about herself and about Diego. Follow the models.

Modelo	Yo soy deportista.

1. _____

2. _____

3. _____

4. _____

5. _____

Modelo	Tú eres paciente.

1. _____

2. _____

3. _____

4. _____

5. _____

Actividad 12

Answer the following questions. Be sure to use the definite or indefinite article where appropriate. Follow the model.

| Modelo | ¿Cómo es tu mamá (*mother*)?

Ella es simpática y graciosa.

1. ¿Cómo eres tú?

_____

2. ¿Cómo es tu profesor(a) de español?

_____

3. ¿Cómo es tu mejor amigo(a)?

_____

4. ¿Cómo es el presidente?

_____

5. ¿Cómo es el director/la directora (*principal*) de tu escuela?

_____

6. ¿Qué te duele?

_____

7. ¿Cuál es la fecha de hoy?

_____

8. ¿Cuál es la fecha del Día de la Independencia?

_____

9. ¿Cuál es tu estación favorita?

_____

10. ¿Qué hora es?

_____

Actividad 13

A reporter for the school newspaper has asked you and several other students in your classroom to submit an article for the paper. The article is about personality traits and activities people like and dislike.

A. Think about your own personality traits. Write four adjectives that describe what you are like and four that describe what you are not like.

SOY   NO SOY

_____   _____

_____   _____

_____   _____

_____   _____

B. Now, write four things that you like to do and four things that you do not like to do.

ME GUSTA   NO ME GUSTA

_____   _____

_____   _____

_____   _____

_____   _____

C. Now, write your article using the information you have compiled about yourself.

_____

_____

_____

_____

_____

_____

_____

_____

_____

_____

_____

Nombre _____   Hora _____

Fecha _____

VIDEO

Antes de ver el video

Actividad 1

Think of two of your favorite and two of your least favorite classes. Write the name of each class, when you have it, and why it is your favorite or least favorite.

Clase	Hora	Comentarios

¿Comprendes?

Actividad 2

Claudia had a bad day. Circle the correct answer to explain what happened to her.

1. Claudia tiene un día difícil en el colegio (*high school*). ¿Por qué?
   a. A Claudia no le gusta su colegio.
   b. Claudia no tiene amigos.
   c. Tiene problemas con el horario.
   d. A Claudia no le gustan las matemáticas.

2. ¿En qué hora tiene Claudia la clase de matemáticas?
   a. en la primera hora   c. en la quinta hora
   b. en la tercera hora   d. todas las anteriores (*all of the above*)

3. Claudia habla con la persona que hace el horario. ¿Cómo se llama?
   a. Sra. Santoro   b. Sr. López   c. Srta. García   d. Sr. Treviño

4. Para Teresa la clase de inglés es
   a. aburrida.   b. interesante.   c. fantástica.   d. difícil.

5. En la tercera hora Claudia piensa que las matemáticas son aburridas, porque
   a. es el primer día de clases.   c. tiene seis clases de matemáticas hoy.
   b. la profesora es muy divertida.   d. no entiende las matemáticas.

Actividad 3

Write **cierto** (*true*) or **falso** (*false*) next to each statement.

1. La clase de matemáticas es muy fácil para Claudia. _____

2. Teresa habla con el Sr. Treviño del problema con su horario. _____

3. Teresa y Claudia tienen el almuerzo a la misma hora. _____

4. Teresa tiene la clase de ciencias sociales en la tercera hora. _____

Y, ¿qué más?

Actividad 4

Complete the paragraph with information about your teachers, classes, school, and friends.

El profesor / La profesora que más me gusta es el Sr. / la Sra. _____ .

Él / Ella enseña la clase de _____ en la _____ hora y su clase

es muy _____ .

Después de la _____ hora tengo el almuerzo. Me gusta mucho porque

puedo estar con _____ y _____ ; ellos / ellas son mis

amigos / amigas.

El director / La directora de mi colegio se llama _____ . Él / Ella es muy

_____ y _____ .

Actividad 5

You overhear several people in the hall trying to find out if they have classes together this year. As you listen to each conversation, write an *X* in the box under *SÍ* if they have a class together, or under *NO* if they do not. You will hear each conversation twice.

	SÍ	NO
1.	_____	_____
2.	_____	_____
3.	_____	_____
4.	_____	_____
5.	_____	_____

Actividad 6

As you stand outside the school counselor's office, you hear four students trying to talk to him. They are all requesting to get out of a certain class. From the part of the conversation that you hear, write in the blank the class from which each student is requesting a transfer. You will hear each statement twice.

	CLASE	PROFESOR(A)
1.	matemáticas	el profesor Pérez
2.	arte	la profesora Muñoz
3.	español	el profesor Cortez
4.	ciencias sociales	la profesora Lenis
5.	almuerzo	
6.	ciencias	el profesor Gala
7.	educación física	el profesor Fernández
8.	inglés	la profesora Ochoa

1. La clase de _____

2. La clase de _____

3. La clase de _____

4. La clase de _____

Realidades ❶

Capítulo 2A

Nombre _____

Hora _____

Fecha _____

AUDIO

Actividad 7

Emilio, a new student from Bolivia, is attending his first pep assembly! He is eager to make friends and begins talking to Diana, who is sitting next to him. Listen to their conversation. If they have something in common, place a check mark in the column labeled **Ellos**. If the statement only applies to Emilio, place a check mark in the column labeled **Él**. If the statement only applies to Diana, place a check mark in the column labeled **Ella**. **Note:** Be sure you have placed a check mark in ONLY one of the columns for each statement. You will hear the conversation twice.

INFORMACIÓN	ÉL	ELLA	ELLOS
Tiene la clase de español en la primera hora.			
Tiene la clase de español en la segunda hora.			
Tiene una profesora simpática.			
Tiene una profesora graciosa.			
Tiene una clase de arte en la quinta hora.			
Tiene una clase de educación física en la quinta hora.			
Practica deportes.			
Estudia mucho en la clase de matemáticas.			
Es trabajador(a).			
Tiene mucha tarea.			
Tiene almuerzo a las once y media.			

Nombre _____ Hora _____

Fecha _____

Actividad 8

Listen as four people talk about what they do during the day. There will be some things that all four people do and other things that not all of them do. Fill in the grid with a check mark if the person says he or she does a certain activity. Also, fill in the **Yo** column with a check mark for the activities that you do every day. You will hear each set of statements twice.

	EVA	DAVID	RAQUEL	JOSÉ	YO

Actividad 9

You and your family are considering hosting a student from Costa Rica for a semester. Before you make the decision, you want to know a little about the student. Listen to part of a recording that the students from Costa Rica made for your class. Use the grid to keep track of what each of the students says. You will then use this information to decide which student would be the most compatible for you and your family. You will hear each set of statements twice.

Estudiante	Característica(s) de la personalidad	Clase favorita	Actividades favoritas
JORGE			
LUZ			
MARCO			
CRISTINA			

Which student is most like you? _____

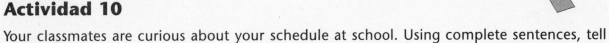

Actividad 10

Your classmates are curious about your schedule at school. Using complete sentences, tell them what classes you have during the day. Follow the model.

Modelo   *Yo tengo la clase de inglés en la segunda hora.* _____

1. _____
2. _____
3. _____
4. _____
5. _____
6. _____
7. _____

Actividad 11

Answer the following questions using the subject pronoun suggested by the pictures. Follow the model.

Modelo   ¿Quiénes usan la computadora?

Ellos usan la computadora. _____ .

¿Quién habla con Teresa?

1. _____ .

¿Quién habla con Paco?

2. _____ .

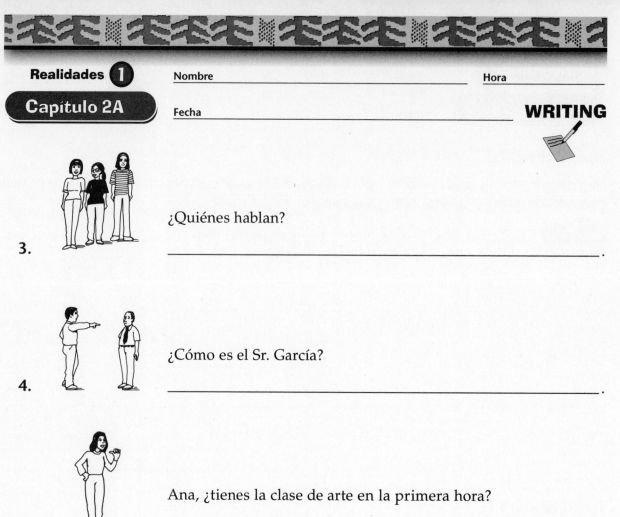

3.

¿Quiénes hablan?

_____.

4.

¿Cómo es el Sr. García?

_____.

5.

Ana

Ana, ¿tienes la clase de arte en la primera hora?

Sí, _____.

6.

Cristina   Yo

¿Cristina y yo somos muy buenas amigas?

Sí, _____.

Actividad 12

A new student at your school has come to you for information about how things work at your school and what your day is like. Answer the student's questions truthfully in complete sentences. Follow the model.

Modelo ¿La secretaria habla mucho por teléfono?

Sí, ella habla mucho _____.

1. ¿Estudias inglés en la primera hora?

_____.

2. ¿Quién enseña la clase de matemáticas?

_____.

3. ¿Necesito un diccionario para la clase de arte?

_____.

4. ¿Cantas en el coro (*choir*)?

_____.

5. ¿Pasas mucho tiempo en la cafetería?

_____.

6. ¿Uds. practican deportes en la clase de educación física?

_____.

7. ¿Los estudiantes usan las computadoras en la clase de ciencias naturales?

_____.

8. ¿Uds. bailan en la clase de español?

_____.

9. ¿Los profesores tocan el piano en la clase de música?

_____.

10. ¿Los estudiantes hablan mucho en la clase de francés?

_____.

WRITING

Actividad 13

A. List two classes that you have, when you have them, and who the teacher is.

Clase	Hora	Profesor(a)
1. _____	_____	_____
2. _____	_____	_____

B. Now, write complete sentences about whether or not you like each class from Part A. Make sure to tell why you do or do not like each class.

Clase 1: _____

_____

_____

_____

Clase 2: _____

_____

_____

_____

C. Now, using the information from Parts A and B, write a paragraph about one of the classes. Make sure to tell the name of the class, when you have it, and who the teacher is. You should also describe your teacher, tell what you do in class, and say whether or not you like the class.

_____

_____

_____

_____

_____

_____

_____

_____

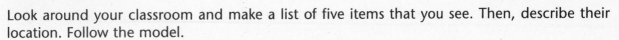

VIDEO

Antes de ver el video

Actividad 1

Look around your classroom and make a list of five items that you see. Then, describe their location. Follow the model.

COSA	DÓNDE ESTÁ
Modelo *la papelera*	*debajo del reloj*
1. _____	_____
2. _____	_____
3. _____	_____
4. _____	_____
5. _____	_____

¿Comprendes?

Actividad 2

Using the screen grabs as clues, answer the following questions with the correct information from the video.

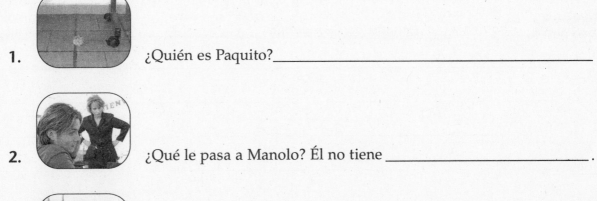

1. ¿Quién es Paquito? _____

2. ¿Qué le pasa a Manolo? Él no tiene _____.

3. ¿Quién tiene el hámster? _____

Realidades 1

Capítulo 2B

Nombre _____

Hora _____

Fecha _____

VIDEO

4. Los estudiantes están en _____.

5. ¿Para qué es el hámster? Es para _____.

Actividad 3

Next to each phrase, write the name of the character who said it in the video.

1. "¿Un ratón en la clase de ciencias sociales? ¡Imposible!" _____

2. "¡No es un ratón! Es mi hámster." _____

3. "Señorita, necesito hablar con usted más tarde." _____

4. "Carlos, no tengo mi tarea." _____

5. "¡Aquí está! Está en mi mochila." _____

6. "Paquito, mi precioso. Ven aquí. ¿Estás bien?" _____

Y, ¿qué más?

Actividad 4

Imagine that Paquito is running around in your classroom. Using the prepositions that you have just learned, indicate four places where he might be. Follow the example below.

| Modelo | *Paquito está encima de la mochila.* |

1. _____

2. _____

3. _____

4. _____

Realidades ❶

Capítulo 2B

Nombre _____

Fecha _____

Hora _____

AUDIO

Actividad 5

As you look at the picture, decide whether the statements you hear are **ciertos** or **falsos**. You will hear each statement twice.

1. cierto   falso
2. cierto   falso
3. cierto   falso
4. cierto   falso
5. cierto   falso

6. cierto   falso
7. cierto   falso
8. cierto   falso
9. cierto   falso
10. cierto   falso

11. cierto   falso
12. cierto   falso
13. cierto   falso
14. cierto   falso
15. cierto   falso

Actividad 6

Tomás suddenly realizes in the middle of his science class that the diskette with his entire class project on it is missing! He asks several people if they know where it is. Listen as different people tell Tomás where they think his diskette is. In the timeline, write what classroom he goes to and where in the classroom he looks, in the order in which you hear them. You will hear this conversation twice.

	Susana	Antonio	Noé	Sr. Atkins
Classroom				
Location in room				

Where did Tomás eventually find his diskette? _____

Actividad 7

It's time to take the Spanish Club picture for the yearbook, but there are several people who have still not arrived. Andrés, the president, decides to use his cell phone to find out where people are. As you listen to the first part of each conversation, complete the sentences below with the information he finds out. For example, you might write: **Beto está en el gimnasio.** You will hear each dialogue twice.

1. Los dos profesores de español _____.

2. Javier _____.

3. Alejandra y Sara _____.

4. Mateo _____.

5. José y Antonieta _____.

Actividad 8

One of your classmates from Spanish class is working in a store that sells school supplies. She overhears a customer speaking Spanish to his father, and decides to try out her Spanish. As she asks him what he wants to buy, she discovers that he never wants just one of anything. As the customer tells your classmate what he wants, write the items on the sales receipt below. Use the pictures below to calculate the price of his purchases. You will hear each conversation twice.

¿QUÉ NECESITA COMPRAR?	PRECIO
Modelo *Tres bolígrafos*	*$6.00*
1.	
2.	
3.	
4.	
5.	
6.	

Realidades 1

Capítulo 2B

Nombre _____

Hora _____

Fecha _____

AUDIO

Actividad 9

Listen to two friends talking outside the door of the Spanish Club meeting. They want to go to the meeting, but they are afraid they won't remember everyone's names. Look at the drawing. In the grid, write in the name of the person who is being described. You will hear each dialogue twice.

(A)	(B)	(C)
(D)	(E)	(F)

Actividad 10

After your first day of school, you are describing your classroom to your parents. Using the picture below, tell them how many of each object there are in the room. Follow the model.

| Modelo | *Hay un escritorio en la sala de clases.* _____ |

1. _____

2. _____

3. _____

4. _____

5. _____

6. _____

7. _____

Actividad 11

You are describing your classroom to your Spanish-speaking pen pal. Using complete sentences and the verb **estar**, tell what is in your room and where each item is located. Follow the model.

Modelo	*Hay una mesa en la clase. Está al lado de la puerta.*

1. _____

2. _____

3. _____

4. _____

5. _____

6. _____

7. _____

8. _____

Actividad 12

Answer the following questions about things you have for school. Use the pictures as a guide. Follow the model.

Modelo	¿Qué hay en la mochila?

En la mochila hay unos lápices y bolígrafos. También hay una calculadora y dos libros: el libro de matemáticas y el libro de inglés.

Realidades **1**

Capítulo 2B

Nombre _____

Fecha _____

Hora _____

WRITING

1. ¿Qué hay en la clase de ciencias sociales?

_____

_____

_____

_____

_____

2. ¿Qué hay encima del escritorio? ¿Y al lado?
¿Y detrás?

_____

_____

_____

_____

_____

Realidades ①

Capítulo 2B

Nombre _____

Fecha _____

Hora _____

WRITING

Actividad 13

The two rooms pictured below were once identical, but Sala 2 has been rearranged. Look at each picture carefully. Circle seven items in Sala 2 that are different from Sala 1. Then, write sentences about how Sala 2 is different. Follow the model.

Sala 1   Sala 2

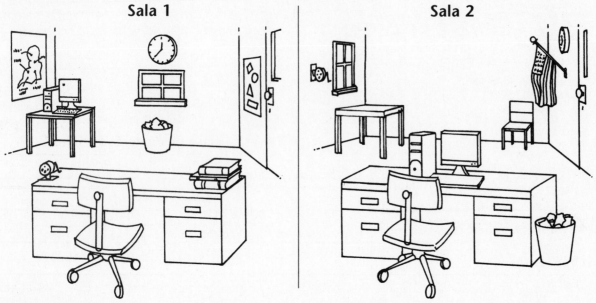

| Modelo | *En la sala 2 no hay libros encima del escritorio.* |

1. _____

_____

2. _____

_____

3. _____

_____

4. _____

_____

5. _____

_____

6. _____

_____

7. _____

_____

Nombre _____ Hora _____

Fecha _____

VIDEO

Antes de ver el video

Actividad 1

What do you like to eat for breakfast and lunch? Fill in the chart with that information.

Desayuno	Almuerzo

¿Comprendes?

Actividad 2

Think about the foods Rosa believes people in the United States eat for breakfast. What do Tomás and Raúl really eat?

1. ¿Qué come Tomás para el desayuno?

   Tomás bebe _____ y come _____ para el desayuno.

2. Y, ¿qué come Raúl?

   Raúl bebe _____ y _____ , come _____ , y a

   veces también come un _____ .

VIDEO

Actividad 3

Although Rosa makes a big breakfast for Tomás that day, the family does not eat very much regularly. Answer the questions below.

1. ¿Quién prepara el desayuno? _____

2. Lorenzo: "Es mucha comida, ¿no? _____ ,
_____ , _____ , _____ ,
_____ ..." Rosa: "En los Estados Unidos, todos comen mucho en el
desayuno."

3. Lorenzo: "Nosotros nunca comemos mucho en el desayuno,
Rosa. Mira, yo sólo bebo un _____ y a veces como
un _____ ."

4. Según Rosa, en los Estados Unidos comemos huevos, salchichas,
tocino y pan tostado en el desayuno y _____
_____ en el almuerzo.

Y, ¿qué más?

Actividad 4

Do you recall what you wrote in **Actividad** 1 about foods that you like to eat? Now that you have heard people in Costa Rica talk about what they eat, write down three questions of your own to ask a classmate about food. With a partner, ask your questions and compare answers.

¿ _____ ?

¿ _____ ?

¿ _____ ?

Nombre _____ Hora _____

Fecha _____ **AUDIO**

Actividad 5

You are helping out a friend at the counter of Restaurante El Gaucho in Argentina. Listen to the orders and record the quantity of each item ordered by each customer in the appropriate box of the chart. You will hear each conversation twice.

RESTAURANTE EL GAUCHO

El almuerzo	Cliente 1	Cliente 2	Cliente 3	Cliente 4
Ensalada				
Hamburguesa				
Hamburguesa con queso				
Sándwich de jamón y queso				
Perro caliente				
Pizza				
Papas fritas				
Refresco				
Té helado				
Galletas				

Nombre _____ Hora _____

Fecha _____

Actividad 6

While working at the Hotel Buena Vista, you need to record breakfast orders for room service. Use the grid to make your report. First, listen carefully for the room number and write it in the appropriate box. Then write in the time requested. Finally, put a check mark next to each item ordered by the person in that room. You will hear each set of statements twice.

HOTEL BUENA VISTA

Número de habitación (*room number*)					
Hora de servicio					
Jugo de naranja					
Jugo de manzana					
Cereal					
Pan tostado					
Huevos					
Jamón					
Tocino					
Salchichas					
Yogur de fresas					
Café					
Café con leche					
Té					

Actividad 7

You are waiting in line at a restaurant counter. You hear people behind you talking about your friends. Listen carefully so you can figure out whom they're talking about. Pay close attention to verb and adjective endings. Put a check mark in the column after each conversation. You will hear each set of statements twice.

	Carlos	Gabriela	Carlos y sus amigos	Gabriela y sus amigas
1.	_____	_____	_____	_____
2.	_____	_____	_____	_____
3.	_____	_____	_____	_____
4.	_____	_____	_____	_____
5.	_____	_____	_____	_____
6.	_____	_____	_____	_____
7.	_____	_____	_____	_____

Actividad 8

Listen as actors from a popular Spanish soap opera are interviewed on the radio program called "**Las dietas de los famosos**" (*Diets of the Famous*). As you listen, write **sí** if the person mentions that he or she eats or drinks something most days. Write **no** if the person says that he or she never eats or drinks the item. You will hear this conversation twice.

	Lana Lote	Óscar Oso	Pepe Pluma	Tita Trompo

Nombre _____

Hora _____

Fecha _____

	Lana Lote	Óscar Oso	Pepe Pluma	Tita Trompo

Realidades ❶

Capítulo 3A

Nombre _____

Hora _____

Fecha _____

AUDIO

Actividad 9

Listen as the woman at the table next to you tries to help a child order from the menu. As you listen, check off the items on the menu that the child says he likes and those he dislikes. Then in the space provided, write what you think would be an "acceptable" lunch for him. You will hear this conversation twice.

le gusta								
no le gusta									

Un almuerzo bueno para Beto es _____

_____ .

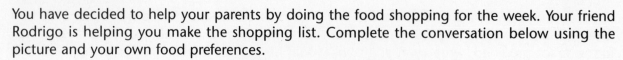

Realidades ❶

Capítulo 3A

Nombre _____

Fecha _____

Hora _____

WRITING

Actividad 10

You have decided to help your parents by doing the food shopping for the week. Your friend Rodrigo is helping you make the shopping list. Complete the conversation below using the picture and your own food preferences.

RODRIGO: ¿Qué hay de beber?

TÚ: _____

RODRIGO: ¿Quieres (*do you want*) algo más?

TÚ: _____

_____

RODRIGO: ¿Qué hay de comer para el desayuno?

TÚ: _____

RODRIGO: ¿Qué más quieres, entonces?

TÚ: _____

_____

RODRIGO: ¿Qué hay para el almuerzo?

TÚ: _____

RODRIGO: ¿Y quieres algo más?

TÚ: _____

_____

RODRIGO: ¿Y qué frutas necesitan?

TÚ : _____

Nombre _____

Hora _____

Fecha _____

WRITING

Actividad 11

Describe each of the following scenes using as many **-er** and **-ir** verbs as you can. Use complete sentences.

_____

_____

_____

_____

yo   Ana y yo

tú   los estudiantes

_____

_____

_____

_____

Actividad 12

In anticipation of your arrival in Spain next week, your host sister writes to ask you about your favorite foods. Complete your response below with sentences using the verbs **gustar** and **encantar**.

Estimada Margarita:

Gracias por su carta. Hay muchas comidas que me gustan. Para el desayuno,

_____. También

_____. Pero no

_____.

Pero me encanta más el almuerzo. Por ejemplo, _____

_____. También

_____. Pero no _____

_____.

¿Y a ti? ¿Te gustan las hamburguesas? ¿ _____

_____? ¿ _____

_____? ¿ _____

_____?

Nos vemos en una semana.

Un fuerte abrazo,

Melinda

Actividad 13

The school nurse is teaching a class on nutrition and asks everyone to fill out a survey about what he or she eats. Using complete sentences, write your responses below.

1. ¿Qué comes y bebes en el desayuno?

_____

_____

_____

_____

_____

2. ¿Qué come y bebe tu familia en el almuerzo?

_____

_____

_____

_____

_____

3. ¿Qué comida te encanta?

_____

_____

_____

_____

_____

Nombre _____ Hora _____

Fecha _____

VIDEO

Antes de ver el video

Actividad 1

Think about the typical diet of a teenager. Which foods are healthy choices and which ones are not? Make a list of five foods in each category.

Comida buena para la salud ☺

Comida mala para la salud ☹

_____   _____

_____   _____

_____   _____

_____   _____

_____   _____

¿Comprendes?

Actividad 2

Write the name of the person from the video who made each statement.

1. "El café de aquí es muy bueno."   _____

2. "No, no; un refresco no; un jugo de fruta."   _____

3. "En Costa Rica, un refresco es un jugo de fruta."   _____

4. "Yo hago mucho ejercicio..."   _____

5. "Aquí en San José, todos caminamos mucho."   _____

6. "... aquí una soda no es una bebida; es un restaurante." _____

7. "Me encanta el gallo pinto."   _____

Actividad 3

Answer the questions.

¿Qué es muy importante para Costa Rica?

1. _____

Según Raúl, ¿qué es bueno de Costa Rica?

2. _____

Según Tomás, ¿qué es bueno para la salud?

3. _____

¿Qué hacen todos en San José?

4. _____

¿Qué más hacen en San José?

5. _____

¿Qué es una *soda* en Costa Rica?

6. _____

Nombre _____ Hora _____

Fecha _____

VIDEO

Y, ¿qué más?

Actividad 4

Tomás was confused because he learned that **un refresco** was a soft drink. However, in Costa Rica **un refresco** is fruit juice. Can you think of any examples of English words that have a different meaning depending on where in the United States you go? What are their different meanings?

_____

_____

_____

_____

_____

_____

_____

Actividad 5

Listen to a radio announcer as he interviews people at the mall about their lifestyles. Pay close attention to the things that they say they do and eat. What in their lifestyles is good or bad for their health? Match what they say to the pictures below. Then write the corresponding letter in the appropriate column. You will hear this conversation twice.

ACTIVIDADES

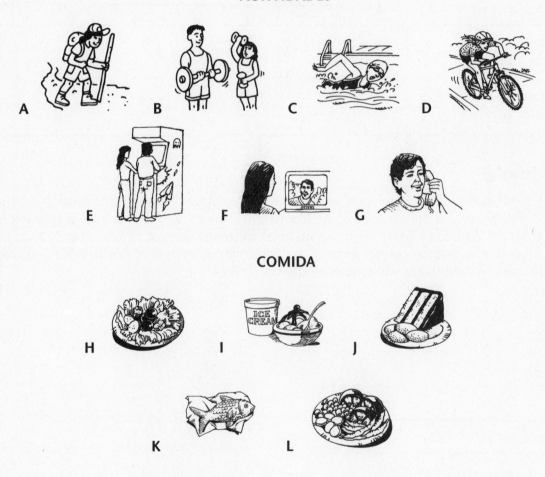

A   B   C   D

E   F   G

COMIDA

H   I   J

K   L

	Bueno para la salud ☺	Malo para la salud ☹
1. Mariana	_____	_____
2. Jorge	_____	_____
3. Luz	_____	_____
4. Nacho	_____	_____

Nombre _____ Hora _____

Fecha _____

AUDIO

Actividad 6

Listen as students in a health class in Costa Rica present a list of the "dos and don'ts" of staying healthy. Which are **consejos lógicos** (*logical advice*) and which are **consejos ridículos** (*ridiculous advice*)? Place a check mark in the appropriate box of the chart. You will hear each set of statements twice.

	1	2	3	4	5	6	7	8	9	10
Consejo lógico										
Consejo ridículo										

Actividad 7

A Spanish-speaking telemarketer calls your home to interview you about the food preferences of teens. He must have gotten your name from your Spanish teacher! He asks you to tell him whether you think certain food items are **malo** or **sabroso**. Be sure to listen carefully so that you will be able to use the correct form of the adjective for each item. Write what you would say in the spaces below. You will hear each question twice.

1. _____

2. _____

3. _____

4. _____

5. _____

6. _____

7. _____

8. _____

9. _____

10. _____

Actividad 8

In an effort to improve food in the school cafeteria, students are asked to anonymously call in their opinions about school food. You are asked to chart the responses of the Spanish-speaking students. As you listen to their opinions, fill in the grid. If they say something positive about a particular menu item, put a plus sign in the appropriate column; if they say something negative, put a minus sign in the column. You will hear each set of statements twice.

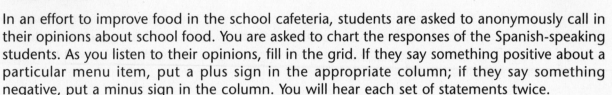

1										
2										
3										
4										
5										

Actividad 9

Listen as people call in to ask Dr. Armando their health questions on his radio program **"Pregunte al doctor Armando."** While you listen to their questions and Dr. Armando's advice (**consejo**), fill in the chart below. Do you agree with his advice? You will hear this conversation twice.

NOMBRE	¿LA PREGUNTA?	EL CONSEJO
1. Beatriz		
2. Mauricio		
3. Loli		
4. Luis		

Realidades ①

Capítulo 3B

Nombre _____

Fecha _____

Hora _____

WRITING

Actividad 10

A. The school nurse has compiled information on what everyone eats and is now telling you which foods are good for your health and which are not. Remember what you wrote for her survey? List the items you eat on a daily basis. Be sure to use words from the previous chapter as well as ones from this chapter.

_____ _____ _____

_____ _____ _____

_____ _____ _____

_____ _____ _____

B. Now, use the nutrition pyramid shown and what you know about a well-balanced diet to fill in what the nurse would say. Follow the model.

Modelo   *Los espaguetis son buenos para la salud. Ud. debe comer mucho pan y*
muchos cereales.

1. _____

_____

2. _____

_____

3. _____

_____

4. _____

_____

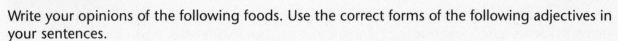
Actividad 11

Write your opinions of the following foods. Use the correct forms of the following adjectives in your sentences.

bueno	malo	sabroso	divertido
malo para la salud		bueno para la salud	
	interesante		horrible

Modelo	*Las uvas son sabrosas.* _____

1. _____

2. _____

3. _____

4. _____

5. _____

6. _____

7. _____

8. _____

Realidades ❶

Capítulo 3B

Nombre _____

Hora _____

Fecha _____

WRITING

Actividad 12

Below you see three groups of friends sitting at tables in a cafeteria. Describe the people and items at each table.

Mesa 1:

_____

_____

_____

_____

Mesa 2:

_____

_____

_____

_____

Mesa 3:

_____

_____

_____

_____

Realidades ❶

Capítulo 3B

Nombre _____

Fecha _____

Hora _____

WRITING

Actividad 13

Write a letter to your Spanish-speaking pen pal about a restaurant that you and your parents like to go to for dinner. Tell what you and your family members normally eat and drink, what the food is like, and what the waiters (**camareros**) are like.

Estimado(a) _____ :

_____

_____

_____

_____

_____

_____

_____

_____

_____

_____

_____

_____

_____

_____

_____

_____

_____

_____

Un abrazo,

_____

Realidades ①

Capítulo 4A

Nombre _____

Hora _____

Fecha _____

VIDEO

Antes de ver el video

Actividad 1

Think of activities you do at different times during the week. Make a list of four activities you do during the week and then four activities you do during the weekend.

Actividades durante la semana

_____

_____

_____

_____

Actividades durante el fin de semana

_____

_____

_____

_____

¿Comprendes?

Actividad 2

Javier has just moved to a new high school in Spain, and he is sitting by himself. Ignacio, Elena, and Ana try to find out more about him. What do they do, and what do they learn? Write **cierto** (*true*) or **falso** (*false*) next to each statement.

1. El estudiante nuevo es un poco reservado. _____

2. Él se llama Gustavo. _____

3. Él es de Salamanca. _____

4. Todos los días va a la biblioteca después de las clases. _____

5. Los tres amigos van a hablar con él. _____

6. A Javier le gusta practicar deportes. _____

Realidades ①

Capítulo 4A

Nombre _____

Hora _____

Fecha _____

VIDEO

7. A veces, él prefiere ir al cine a ver películas. _____

8. A él no le gusta hablar con su amigo Esteban de San Antonio. _____

Actividad 3

What do the new friends do after class? Fill the blanks with complete sentences.

Nuevos amigos	¿Adónde va después de las clases?
1. Javier	
2. Ignacio	
3. Elena	
4. Ana	

Y, ¿qué más?

Actividad 4

What do you do after school every day? What do you sometimes do, and what do you never do at all? Write a short paragraph about your afterschool activities, following the example below.

Modelo *Yo voy a mi trabajo todos los días en el centro comercial. A veces, voy con una amiga al cine después del trabajo. Nunca voy al gimnasio durante la semana.*

_____

_____

Nombre _____ Hora _____

Fecha _____ **AUDIO**

Actividad 5

Listen as Lorena talks to Luis and Antonio about where they are going during the week. Under each picture in the grid, write in the name of Luis or Antonio if they tell Lorena they are going to that place. In some cases, you will fill in both of their names. After completing the grid, you will be able to complete the sentences under the grid. You will hear this conversation twice.

lunes							
martes							
miércoles							
jueves							
viernes							
sábado							
domingo							

1. Luis y Antonio van al (a la) _____ el _____ .

2. También van al (a la) _____ el _____ .

Realidades ❶

Capítulo 4A

Nombre _____

Hora _____

Fecha _____

AUDIO

Actividad 6

You are volunteering as a tour guide during the upcoming Hispanic Arts Festival in your community. To make sure you would be able to understand the following questions if a visitor were to ask them, write the number of the question under the correct picture that would correspond to a logical response. You can check your answers to see if you're ready to answer visitors' questions during the Festival. You will hear each question twice.

Actividad 7

Your friend Miguel calls his mother from your house to give her an update on his plans for the day. Just from listening to his side of the conversation, you realize that his mother has LOTS of questions. What does she ask him, based on Miguel's answers? Choose from the following:

A. ¿Adónde vas?

B. ¿Con quiénes vas?

C. ¿Cuándo vas?

D. ¿Cómo es tu amigo?

E. ¿Por qué van?

You will hear each set of statements twice.

1. _____   2. _____   3. _____   4. _____   5. _____

Actividad 8

The yearbook staff is identifying students' pictures for the yearbook. Look at the pictures from the class trip to Mexico. Listen to the conversations and write the names of Arturo, Susi, Gloria, Martín, David, Eugenia, Enrique, and Lucía under the correct pictures. You will hear each dialogue twice.

_____   _____   _____

_____   _____   _____

Actividad 9

Listen as a radio interviewer talks to Maricela, a young woman from Spain, about her city that was once home to the **Reyes** Fernando and Isabel. You will learn why it is such a popular tourist spot. After listening, answer the questions below. You will hear this conversation twice.

1. Maricela es de
   a) Madrid.   b) Aranjuez.   c) Barcelona.

2. La ciudad es famosa por
   a) el pescado.   b) el helado.   c) las fresas.

3. Los turistas van
   a) al palacio.   b) a las montañas.   c) a la playa.

4. La ciudad de Maricela está a unos _____ minutos de Madrid.
   a) quince   b) treinta   c) cincuenta

5. Las comidas típicas son
   a) pizza y espaguetis.   b) fresas y pasteles de manzana.   c) pollo y judías verdes.

6. Maricela va _____ para pasar tiempo con los amigos.
   a) al parque   b) al cine   c) a las montañas

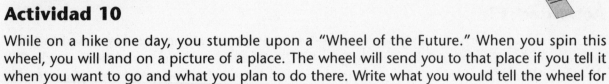

Actividad 10

While on a hike one day, you stumble upon a "Wheel of the Future." When you spin this wheel, you will land on a picture of a place. The wheel will send you to that place if you tell it when you want to go and what you plan to do there. Write what you would tell the wheel for each place. Follow the model.

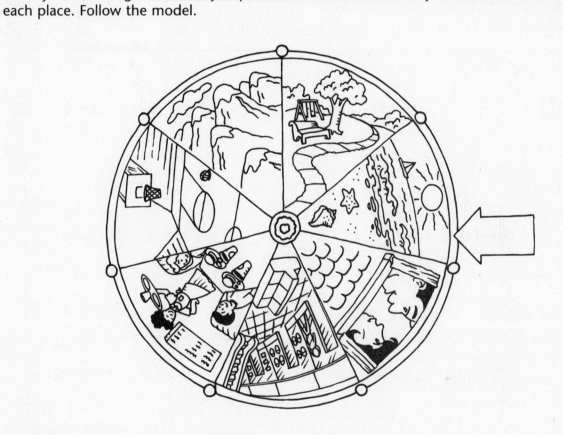

| Modelo | *Voy a la playa el viernes para nadar.* _____ |

1. _____

2. _____

3. _____

4. _____

5. _____

6. _____

7. _____

Realidades ❶

Capítulo 4A

Nombre _____

Fecha _____

Hora _____

WRITING

Actividad 11

You are having a surprise party for your best friend next weekend, and you need to know where your family and friends are going to be this week so that you can get in touch with them to make plans. Below is a planner containing information on everyone's plans for the week. Using the pictures to help you, write where your friends and family will be and what they will be doing on that day. Use the model as a guide.

Modelo Lunes: _El lunes yo voy a la biblioteca para hacer la tarea._

YO

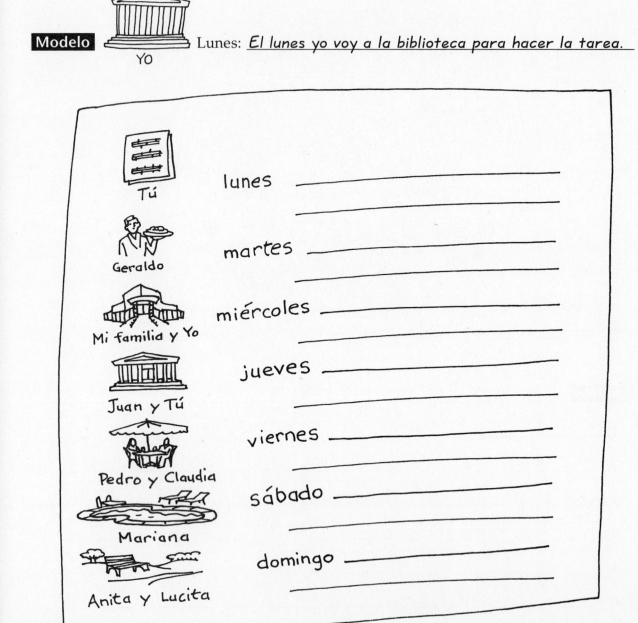

Tú

lunes _____

Geraldo

martes _____

Mi familia y Yo

miércoles _____

Juan y Tú

jueves _____

Pedro y Claudia

viernes _____

Mariana

sábado _____

Anita y Lucita

domingo _____

Actividad 12

You are a contestant on a game show. The host of the show has given you these answers. Write the corresponding questions.

Modelo   El catorce de febrero

        ¿Cuándo es el Día de San Valentín?

1. El primer presidente de los Estados Unidos

   _____

2. Al norte (*north*) de los Estados Unidos

   _____

3. Usamos esta cosa para conectar al Internet.

   _____

4. Muy bien, gracias. ¿Y tú?

   _____

5. Vamos a la tienda para comprar frutas.

   _____

6. Las personas que enseñan las clases

   _____

7. Usamos estas partes del cuerpo para ver.

   _____

Actividad 13

A. Write four complete sentences that tell about places you and a friend go to on the weekend.

1. _____

2. _____

3. _____

4. _____

Realidades ❶

Capítulo 4A

Nombre _____

Hora _____

Fecha _____

WRITING

B. Now, use your sentences from Part A to write a paragraph telling with whom you go to these places, what the places are like, and what you do when you are there.

_____

_____

_____

_____

_____

_____

_____

_____

_____

_____

_____

_____

_____

Antes de ver el video

Actividad 1

Think of activities you like to do. Here is a list of six activities. Rank them in order from your favorite to your least favorite, with 1 as your favorite and 6 as your least favorite.

_____ ir a bailar   _____ ir al cine a ver películas

_____ nadar   _____ montar en bicicleta

_____ estudiar en la biblioteca _____ ir de compras al centro comercial

¿Comprendes?

Actividad 2

Ignacio, Javier, Elena, and Ana are playing soccer at the park. Who makes each statement? Write the name of the person who says each item on the line.

1. "Mañana juego al tenis con mis primos."   _____

2. "Yo también estoy muy cansada y tengo mucha sed."   _____

3. "Prefiero otros deportes, como el fútbol."   _____

4. "¿Sabes jugar también al vóleibol?"   _____

5. "También me gusta ir de pesca."   _____

6. "Puedes bailar conmigo…"   _____

7. "Lo siento. No sé bailar bien."   _____

8. "Voy a preparar un pastel fabuloso."   _____

Realidades ①

Capítulo 4B

Nombre _____

Hora _____

Fecha _____

VIDEO

Actividad 3

Look at the activities below, and circle the ones you saw or heard about while watching the video. Then, write the ones that Elena can do well on the lines below.

jugar al fútbol	jugar al tenis	ir de cámping	ir de pesca
	ir a las fiestas	ver el partido	jugar al vóleibol	
caminar en el parque		jugar al fútbol americano		practicar deportes
ir al concierto	preparar un pastel	jugar al béisbol	jugar al golf
	jugar al básquetbol	bailar y cantar	tomar refrescos	

_____

_____

Y, ¿qué mas?

Actividad 4

Imagine that Ignacio, Javier, Elena, and Ana want you to join them in their various activities. What answers might you give them? Respond to their invitations with some of the phrases from the video, or make up your own responses from what you have learned. Follow the model.

Modelo   ¿Quieres jugar al fútbol en el parque?

Sí, quiero jugar al fútbol en el parque, pero no juego muy bien.

1. ¿Puedes jugar al tenis mañana?

_____

2. Oye, juegas muy bien al vóleibol. ¿Puedes jugar más tarde?

_____

3. ¿Quieres ir con nosotros a la fiesta esta noche?

_____

4. ¿Sabes bailar?

_____

Realidades ❶

Capítulo 4B

Nombre _____ Hora _____

Fecha _____

AUDIO

Actividad 5

There are not enough hours in the day to do everything we want to do. Listen to the following interviews. What do these people want more time to do? In the blanks provided, write the number of the statement that corresponds to each picture. You will hear each set of statements twice.

Actividad 6

After listening to each of the following statements, decide if you think the excuses given are believable (**creíble**) or unbelievable (**increíble**). Be prepared to defend your answers with a partner after making your decisions. You will hear each set of statements twice.

EXCUSAS, EXCUSAS

	Creíble	Increíble		Creíble	Increíble
1.	☐	☐	5.	☐	☐
2.	☐	☐	6.	☐	☐
3.	☐	☐	7.	☐	☐
4.	☐	☐	8.	☐	☐

Realidades 1

Capítulo 4B

Nombre _____

Hora _____

Fecha _____

AUDIO

Actividad 7

Listen to the following couple as they try to decide what they are going to do tonight. Every time an activity is mentioned that one of the two people is going to do, draw a circle around the picture. If the other person is NOT going to do that activity, draw an *X* through the picture. The pictures with circles only should represent what both people finally decide to do. You will hear each conversation twice.

Actividad 8

Listen as a radio program host interviews a fitness expert, doctora Benítez, about the best way to get in shape. Listen to the **entrevista** (*interview*), and choose the best answer to the questions below. You will hear this conversation twice.

1. ¿En qué es experta la doctora Benítez?

    a) deportes   b) cocinar   c) música   d) ejercicio y nutrición

2. Según la doctora, ¿cuántos minutos de ejercicio debes hacer todos los días?

    a) una hora   b) quince minutos   c) treinta minutos

3. Según Miguel, ¿por qué no puede hacer mucho ejercicio?

    a) Es demasiado perezoso.   b) Está muy ocupado.   c) Está triste.

4. ¿Qué es divertido para Miguel?

    a) jugar al tenis   b) ver la tele   c) jugar al fútbol

5. Después de jugar, ¿qué no debemos comer?

    a) cereales   b) frutas y verduras   c) pasteles

Realidades ①

Capítulo 4B

Nombre _____

Hora _____

Fecha _____

AUDIO

Actividad 9

Your Spanish teacher always encourages you to speak Spanish to your classmates outside of class. In order to do that, you and your friends agreed to talk on the phone and/or leave messages on each other's answering machines for at least a week. Listen to the messages your friends have left on your answering machine today. Based on the messages, decide a) where the person wants to go; b) what the person wants to do; c) what time the person wants to go. Use the chart below to record the information. You will hear each set of statements twice.

	¿Adónde quiere ir?	¿Qué quiere hacer?	¿A qué hora quiere ir?
Justo			
Eva			
José			
Margarita			
Pedro			

Actividad 10

A. Read the following announcements of upcoming events in Madrid. Underneath each announcement, write whether or not you are going to each event and why or why not.

UNA NOCHE DE ÓPERA ITALIANA	PARTIDO DE FÚTBOL
PRESENTANDO a **JOSÉ CARRERAS** en el Auditorio Nacional de Música, Madrid	REAL BETIS CONTRA REAL MADRID
el viernes a las siete de la noche	el domingo a las dos de la tarde en el Estadio Santiago Bernabeu

_____   _____

_____   _____

Fiesta Deportiva

¿Te gusta practicar deportes? ¿Eres atlético?

Ven a mi fiesta deportiva y puedes jugar varios deportes
con muchas personas.

La fiesta es desde el viernes a las cinco de la tarde hasta
el lunes a las cinco de la mañana.

_____

B. Now, in the spaces below, write whether five people you know are going to any one of the events and why or why not. Follow the model.

Modelo   *Mi amiga Ana va al partido de fútbol porque le gusta mucho el fútbol.*

   Mi amigo Ronaldo no va al concierto porque no le gusta la ópera.

1. _____

2. _____

3. _____

4. _____

5. _____

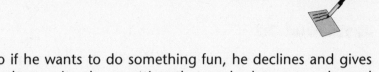

Actividad 11

Every time a classmate asks Eugenio if he wants to do something fun, he declines and gives a different excuse. In the spaces below, write the question that each classmate asks and Eugenio's varying answers. Follow the model.

Modelo

—*¿Vas a levantar pesas conmigo?* _____

—*No, no puedo levantar pesas porque me duele la cabeza.*

1. —¿ _____ ?

   —No, _____ .

2. —¿ _____ ?

   —No, _____ .

3. —¿ _____ ?

   —No, _____ .

4. —¿ _____ ?

   —No, _____ .

5. —¿ _____ ?

   —No, _____ .

6. —¿ _____ ?

   —No, _____ .

7. —¿ _____ ?

   —No, _____ .

Nombre _____ Hora _____

Fecha _____

Actividad 12

When put in the right order, each set of blocks below will ask a question. Unscramble the blocks by writing the contents of each block in the blank boxes. Then, answer the questions in the space provided.

1.

JUEG	DE	EPOR	OS F	UÉ	D	AS	L

INES	¿A Q	TES	NA?	SEMA

_____

_____

2.

¿A Q	MIGO	TES	US A	JUEG	UÉ D

S?	AN T	EPOR

_____

_____

3.

GA?	L ES	FAVO	¿CUÁ	RITO	JUE

RTE	UIÉN	Y Q	TU	DEPO

_____

_____

Realidades ❶

Capítulo 4B

Nombre _____

Hora _____

Fecha _____

WRITING

Actividad 13

You are having a mid-semester party.

A. First, fill in the invitation below with the information about your party.

FIESTA DE MEDIO SEMESTRE

Lugar: _____

Hora: _____

Comida: _____

_____

RSVP: _____

B. Since you don't have everyone's mailing address, you have to e-mail some people about the party. Write your e-mail below. In addition to inviting them, tell them what activities you will have at the party, and where your house is (**está cerca de la biblioteca**, etc.).

```
Estimados amigos:

    _____
_____
_____
_____
    _____
    _____
_____
_____
    _____

¡Me gustaría ver a todos en la fiesta!

                                    Un fuerte abrazo,

                                    _____
```

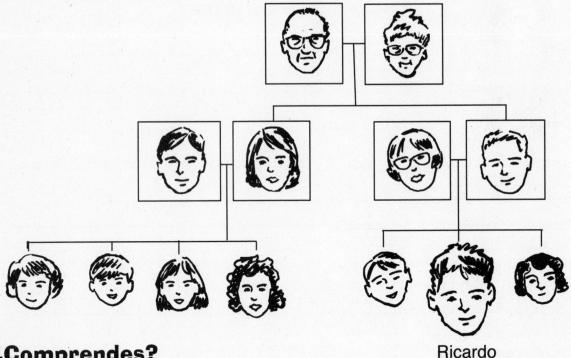

Realidades ❶

Capítulo 5A

Nombre _____

Hora _____

Fecha _____

VIDEO

Antes de ver el video

Actividad 1

Look at this family tree. Label each person with his or her relationship to Ricardo.

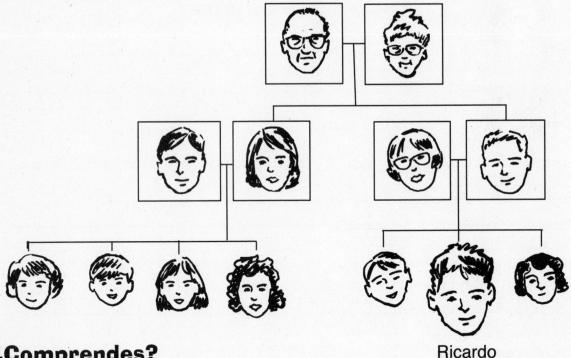

Ricardo

¿Comprendes?

Actividad 2

Cristina had a birthday party with some of her family members. How much do you remember about that party? Write **cierto** or **falso** next to each statement.

1. Angélica hace un video de la fiesta de su hermano. _____

2. El papá de Cristina saca fotos de la fiesta. _____

3. A Gabriel le gustan los deportes. _____

4. El perro de Cristina se llama Piñata. _____

5. La abuela de Cristina decora la fiesta con papel picado. _____

6. Capitán es muy sociable, le encanta estar con la familia. _____

7. Carolina es la hermana de Gabriel y Angélica. _____

8. Ricardo es el abuelo de Esteban. _____

Actividad 3

Who is being described? Write his or her name next to the description.

Description	Name

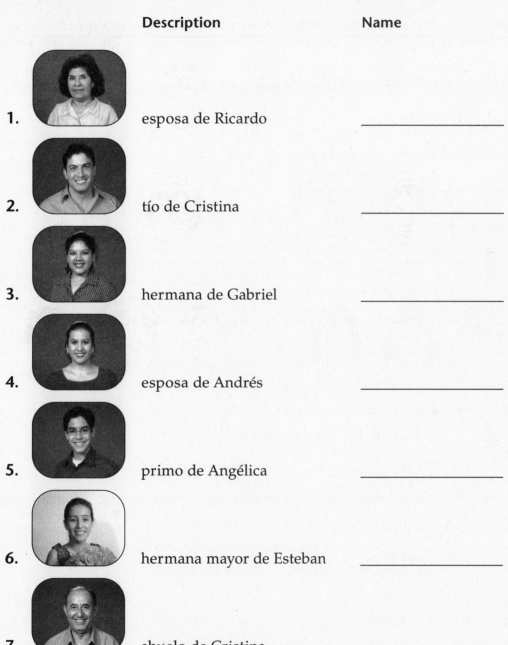

1. esposa de Ricardo   _____

2. tío de Cristina   _____

3. hermana de Gabriel   _____

4. esposa de Andrés   _____

5. primo de Angélica   _____

6. hermana mayor de Esteban   _____

7. abuelo de Cristina   _____

VIDEO

Y, ¿qué más?

Actividad 4

At Cristina's party we met many family members. Why don't you introduce your family, too?
Write three sentences about your family or a family you know well. Follow the examples below.

Yo vivo en mi casa con mi mamá y mi hermano.

TÚ: _____

Mi hermano se llama Martín y tiene 10 años.

TÚ: _____

Yo tengo muchos primos y primas.

TÚ: _____

The lyrics for "Las mañanitas" as sung on the video are:

Éstas son las mañanitas que cantaba el rey David
a las muchachas bonitas, te las cantamos a ti.
Despierta, mi bien, despierta, mira que ya amaneció,
ya los pajarillos cantan, la luna ya se metió.

These are the early morning birthday songs
that King David used to sing
to pretty girls, and so we sing them to you.
Wake up, my dear, wake up, look, dawn has already come,
the little birds are singing, the moon is gone.

Actividad 5

Beto is showing Raúl a picture of his family at a birthday party. Identify as many people as you can and write their names and relationship to Beto under the pictures. If Beto refers to a pet, simply write the pet's name under the picture. You will hear this conversation twice.

_____   _____   _____

_____   _____   _____

_____   _____   _____

_____   _____   _____

_____   _____   _____

_____   _____   _____

Realidades ❶

Capítulo 5A

Nombre _____

Hora _____

Fecha _____

AUDIO

Actividad 6

You are chosen to participate in a popular radio quiz show on a local Spanish radio station. When it is your turn, you are happy to hear that your questions are in the category of **FAMILIA**. See if you can answer all of the questions correctly on the entry card below. Each question becomes a little more difficult. You will hear each set of questions twice.

1. _____

2. _____

3. _____

4. _____

5. _____

Actividad 7

Listen as three brothers talk to their mother after school. Try to fill in all of the squares in the grid with the correct information about Julio, Mateo, and Víctor. Remember, you might not hear the information given in the same order as it appears in the grid. You will hear this conversation twice.

	¿Cuántos años tiene?	¿Qué le gusta hacer?	¿Qué tiene que hacer?	¿Qué tiene en la mochila?
Julio				
Mateo				
Víctor				

Nombre _____

Hora _____

Fecha _____

Actividad 8

Listen as two students tell their host families in Chile about their own families back home. As you listen to both of them, see if you can tell which family is being described. Put a check mark in the appropriate box on the grid. You will hear each set of statements twice.

La familia Gómez

La familia Sora

	1	2	3	4	5	6	7	8
La familia Gómez								
La familia Sora								

Realidades 1

Capítulo 5A

Nombre _____

Hora _____

Fecha _____

AUDIO

Actividad 9

Listen to the following phone calls to Ana, a favorite local talk show host. Each caller has a problem with someone in his or her family. As you listen to each caller, take notes on his or her problems. After all of the callers have spoken, write a sentence of advice for each caller. You may write your advice in English. You will hear set of statements twice.

	PROBLEMA	CONSEJO
Maritza	_____	_____
	_____	_____
	_____	_____
	_____	_____
Armando	_____	_____
	_____	_____
	_____	_____
	_____	_____
Andrés	_____	_____
	_____	_____
	_____	_____
	_____	_____
María Luisa	_____	_____
	_____	_____
	_____	_____
	_____	_____

Actividad 10

Look at the pages from the Rulfo family photo album below. Then, write one or two sentences describing the people in each photo. What is their relationship to each other? What do you think they are like, based on the pictures?

Juanito, Lolita y Pepe

Pepe, Marcos, Romana, Timoteo y Luisita

"El cumpleaños de Rafael"

1. Foto 1

_____

_____

_____

2. Foto 2

_____

_____

_____

3. Foto 3

_____

_____

_____

Actividad 11

People have many obligations during the day. Using **tener que**, write what you think the following people have to do at the time of day or place given. Follow the model.

Modelo   mi padre / a las 7:00 de la mañana

Mi padre tiene que desayunar a las siete de la mañana.

1. yo / a las 7:30 de la mañana

   _____

2. tú / en la clase de español

   _____

3. los estudiantes / en la clase de inglés

   _____

4. el profesor / en la clase de matemáticas

   _____

5. las personas de la escuela / a las doce de la tarde (al mediodía)

   _____

6. Uds. / en la clase de arte

   _____

7. los estudiantes malos / en la clase de educación física

   _____

8. mi amigo / a las 3:00 de la tarde

   _____

9. mis hermanos y yo / a las 5:00 de la tarde

   _____

10. mi familia / a las 6:00 de la tarde

    _____

Actividad 12

A. Your family tree is very complex. It takes many links to connect everyone in the family. Using possessive adjectives, write 10 sentences about how people are related in your family. Use the model to help you.

Modelo   *Mi tío tiene dos hijos.*

          Mi abuelo es el padre de mi tía.

1. _____

2. _____

3. _____

4. _____

5. _____

6. _____

7. _____

8. _____

9. _____

10. _____

B. Now, draw your family tree.

Actividad 13

Your pen pal from Argentina has asked you to tell her about a member of your family. First, tell her the person's name, age, and relationship to you. Then, describe what the person is like.

Once you finish writing, read your description and check to make sure that all the words are spelled correctly and that you have used accents where necessary. Also, check to make sure the endings of the adjectives agree with the nouns they are describing.

Hola, Ana Sofía:

_____

_____

_____

_____

_____

_____

_____

_____

_____

_____

Saludos,

_____

Realidades ❶

Capítulo 5B

Nombre _____

Hora _____

Fecha _____

VIDEO

Antes de ver el video

Actividad 1

Select from the word bank the appropriate nouns to write under each heading: things needed to set the table, things to eat, and things to drink.

menú	tacos	tenedor	flan
enchiladas	limonada	servilleta	postre
café	refresco	cuchillo	jugo de naranja

Para poner la mesa

_____

_____

_____

_____

Para comer

_____

_____

_____

_____

Para beber

_____

_____

_____

_____

¿Comprendes?

Actividad 2

Angélica's family is having dinner at the restaurant **México Lindo**. Find the best choice to complete each statement by writing the letter in the space provided.

1. El camarero está nervioso; _____

   a. tiene mucho trabajo.

   b. es su primer día de trabajo.

   c. tiene sueño.

2. El papá de Angélica pide un té helado _____

   a. porque tiene calor.

   b. porque es delicioso.

   c. porque tiene frío.

Realidades ❶

Capítulo 5B

Nombre _____

Hora _____

Fecha _____

VIDEO

3. La mamá de Angélica pide de postre _____

   a. arroz con pollo.

   b. tacos de bistec.

   c. flan.

4. La mamá de Angélica necesita _____

   a. una servilleta.

   b. el menú.

   c. un cuchillo y un tenedor.

Actividad 3

Match each person with the things he or she ordered. Write the letter of the foods and beverages in the spaces provided.

1. Mamá _____

   a. jugo de naranja y fajitas de pollo

2. Angélica _____

   b. enchiladas

3. Papá _____

   c. café, ensalada de frutas y flan

4. Esteban _____

   d. té helado, tacos de bistec y café

5. Cristina _____

   e. refresco y arroz con pollo

6. Sr. del pelo castaño _____

   f. hamburguesa y refresco

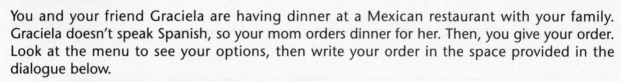

Realidades ❶

Capítulo 5B

Nombre _____

Hora _____

Fecha _____

VIDEO

Y, ¿qué más?

Actividad 4

You and your friend Graciela are having dinner at a Mexican restaurant with your family. Graciela doesn't speak Spanish, so your mom orders dinner for her. Then, you give your order. Look at the menu to see your options, then write your order in the space provided in the dialogue below.

	MENÚ	
BEBIDAS	**PLATO PRINCIPAL**	**POSTRES**
Refrescos	Enchiladas	Flan
Jugo de naranja	Tacos de carne/pollo	Helado
Té helado/caliente	Fajitas de carne/pollo	Frutas frescas
Café	Burritos	

CAMARERO: ¿Qué van a pedir para beber?

MAMÁ: La joven quiere un jugo de naranja, y yo quiero un refresco.

TÚ: _____

CAMARERO: ¿Qué quieren pedir para el plato principal?

MAMÁ: Para la joven enchiladas, y yo quiero arroz con pollo.

TÚ: _____

CAMARERO: ¿Quieren pedir algo de postre?

MAMÁ: Para la joven un flan. Yo no quiero nada, gracias.

TÚ: _____

Realidades 1

Capítulo 5B

Nombre _____

Hora _____

Fecha _____

AUDIO

Actividad 5

You are delighted to find out that you can understand a conversation that a family at a table near you in a restaurant is having in Spanish. The family doesn't seem very happy with the waiter. Listen to find out what each family member is upset about. By looking at the pictures in the grid below, check off the item that is causing the problem. You will hear each conversation twice.

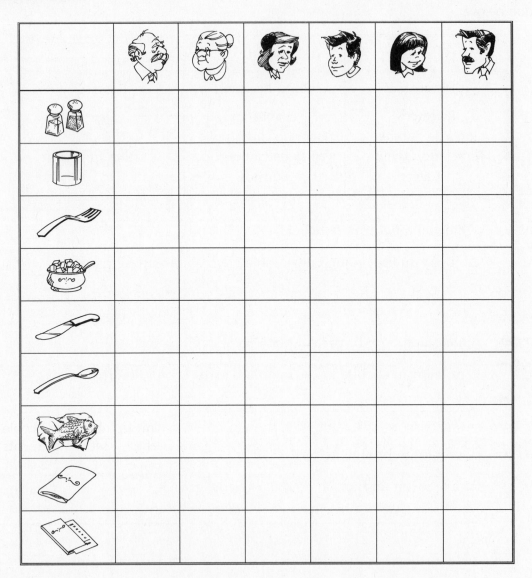

Actividad 6

Five young people go to a department store to buy hats (**sombreros**) as presents for their friends. Listen as each person describes the person he or she is buying the present for. Write the name of each person described under the hat that best matches that person. You will hear each conversation twice.

Realidades 1

Capítulo 5B

Nombre _____

Hora _____

Fecha _____

AUDIO

sociable, deportista, atrevido(a)
_____

romántico(a), talentoso(a), paciente
_____

serio(a), trabajador(a), práctico(a)
_____

elegante, divertido(a), simpático(a)
_____

aventurero(a), atrevido(a), interesante
_____

Actividad 7

Listen as a group of friends discuss Julia's upcoming surprise birthday party. Look at the list of party items. Write the name of each person next to the item that he or she is bringing. Circle any item that still needs to be assigned. You will hear this conversation twice.

Los platos _____	Los refrescos _____	Las servilletas _____
Los vasos _____	Los globos _____	El postre _____
Los tenedores _____	La piñata _____	Las flores _____
Las cucharas _____	Las luces _____	El helado _____

Actividad 8

Iván knows many different people from various places. Listen to him describe these people. Fill in the chart as you hear each piece of information given. You will hear each set of statements twice.

	¿De dónde es/son?	¿Dónde está(n)?	¿Está(n) contento/a/os/as?
Juanita			
Los tíos			
Iván y su familia			
Felipe			
Juanita y Julie			

Nombre _____ Hora _____

Fecha _____

AUDIO

Actividad 9

Listen as a girl describes a photo of a party to her friend who was unable to attend. Write the names of each person described on the line that corresponds to each picture. You will hear the dialogues twice.

A. _____   D. _____

B. _____   E. _____

C. _____   F. _____

Actividad 10

Draw a picture of yourself and three other people in your family. Then, write a description of the person below each picture. You can draw imaginary family members if you prefer.

1.

Yo
_____

_____
_____
_____
_____
_____
_____
_____

2.

_____

_____
_____
_____
_____
_____
_____
_____

3.

_____

_____
_____
_____
_____
_____
_____
_____

4.

_____

_____
_____
_____
_____
_____
_____
_____

Realidades 1

Capítulo 5B

Nombre _____

Hora _____

Fecha _____

WRITING

Actividad 11

In preparation for their upcoming party, Juan and Elisa are talking on the phone about who is coming and what each guest is bringing. Read Elisa's guest list below, then complete the friends' conversation by writing sentences that include the correct form of either **venir** or **traer**.

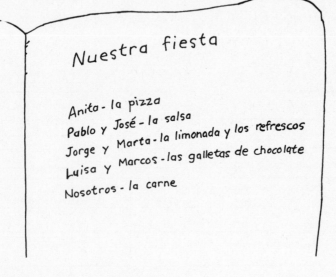

Nuestra fiesta

Anita - la pizza
Pablo y José - la salsa
Jorge y Marta - la limonada y los refrescos
Luisa y Marcos - las galletas de chocolate
Nosotros - la carne

JUAN: ¿Anita viene a la fiesta el sábado?

ELISA: _____.

JUAN: ¡Qué bien! ¿También van a venir Pablo y José?

ELISA: Sí. Ellos _____.

JUAN: ¿Qué traen ellos?

ELISA: _____.

JUAN: Bien. Y ¿quién trae las bebidas?

ELISA: Pues, _____.

JUAN: Sí. Ahora, ¿quiénes traen el postre?

ELISA: _____.

JUAN: ¡Perfecto! ¿Y nosotros? ¿_____?

ELISA: ¡Traemos la carne, por supuesto!

Realidades ❶

Capítulo 5B

Nombre

Hora

Fecha

WRITING

Actividad 12

Describe the following people. Consider their mood and location, their personality and appearance. Be creative and use the pictures and model to help you.

Modelo

Él es joven. Su pelo es corto y negro.

Es un chico estudioso.

Está en casa ahora porque está enfermo.

1. _____

2. _____

3. _____

4. _____

Realidades 1

Capítulo 5B

Nombre _____

Hora _____

Fecha _____

WRITING

Actividad 13

There is going to be a picnic at your new house, and your mother is telling you who is coming and what he or she will be bringing. Write what your mother says, using a name, a description word, and an item from the columns below. Use either **venir** or **traer** in your sentence. Use the names only once. Follow the model.

Nombre	Descripción	Va a traer
Los Sres. Vázquez	viejo	platos
	joven	tenedores
La Srta. Espinosa	contento	vasos
	simpático	pollo
Antonio Jerez	artístico	hamburguesas
	pelirrojo	pasteles
Fernando y María Sosa	enfermo	servilletas
	guapo	limonada
Catalina de la Cuesta	alto	cuchillos
	bajo	tazas

Modelo   *La señorita Espinosa viene a la fiesta. Ella es la mujer joven y simpática que vive cerca de nuestra casa. Ella siempre está contenta y trae los pasteles.*

1. _____

_____

2. _____

_____

3. _____

_____

4. _____

_____

Realidades ①

Capítulo 6A

Nombre _____

Fecha _____

Hora _____

VIDEO

Antes de ver el video

Actividad 1

Make a list of five items in your bedroom and five adjectives that describe your bedroom.

Cosas en mi dormitorio

_____

_____

_____

_____

_____

Descripción de mi dormitorio

_____

_____

_____

_____

_____

¿Comprendes?

Actividad 2

Below are some words and phrases that you have learned so far. On the lines below, write only the words that you most likely heard in the video episode about Ignacio's room.

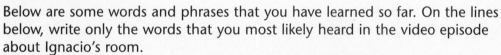

a veces	ratón	bistec	¿A qué hora?	almuerzo
foto	desordenado	lámpara	pequeños	estante
pared	bueno	casa	mochila	peor
abuelos	bailar	cuarto	bicicleta	escritorio
calculadora	¿Adónde?	fiesta	discos compactos	color

_____   _____   _____

_____   _____   _____

_____   _____   _____

_____   _____   _____

_____   _____   _____

_____   _____   _____

Nombre _____

Hora _____

Fecha _____

VIDEO

Actividad 3

Put the following scenes from the video in chronological order by numbering them from 1–7.

Nombre _____   Hora _____

Fecha _____

VIDEO

Y, ¿qué más?

Actividad 4

What is your room like? Is it messy or neat? What do you have to the left and to the right of the room? What do you have on the wall, on the nightstand, or on a bookshelf? Can you compare your room to someone else's? Describe your room, using as much new vocabulary as you can. Follow the sample paragraph below.

Modelo

Mi cuarto es menos ordenado que el cuarto de mi hermana. A la izquierda tengo un estante, muy desordenado, con discos compactos. A la derecha está mi escritorio con libros y revistas. Tengo una foto de mi familia en la pared. También tengo otra foto de mi hermana en su cuarto, ¡y está ordenado!

_____

_____

_____

_____

_____

_____

Realidades ❶

Capítulo 6A

Nombre _____

Fecha _____

Hora _____

AUDIO

Actividad 5

Marta and her sister Ana have very similar bedrooms. However, since they have unique personalities and tastes, there are some differences! For each statement you hear, check off in the appropriate column whose bedroom is being described. You will hear each statement twice.

El dormitorio de Marta

El dormitorio de Ana

	Marta	Ana			Marta	Ana
1.	☐	☐	6.		☐	☐
2.	☐	☐	7.		☐	☐
3.	☐	☐	8.		☐	☐
4.	☐	☐	9.		☐	☐
5.	☐	☐	10.		☐	☐

Realidades 1

Capítulo 6A

Nombre _____

Hora _____

Fecha _____

AUDIO

Actividad 6

Your Spanish teacher asks you to represent your school at a local university's **Competencia Escolar** (*Scholastic Competition*) for secondary Spanish students. She gives you a tape to practice with for the competition. As you listen to the recording, decide whether the statement is true or false and mark it in the grid. You will hear each set of statements twice.

	1	2	3	4	5	6	7	8	9	10
Cierto										
Falso										

Actividad 7

Sra. Harding's class is planning an Immersion Weekend for the school district's Spanish students. Listen as four committee members discuss the best food to have, the best activities for younger and older students, and the best colors for the t-shirt (**camiseta**) that will be given to all participants. To keep track of what everyone thinks, fill in the grid. You will hear each set of statements twice.

	La mejor comida	Las actividades para los estudiantes menores	Las actividades para los estudiantes mayores	El mejor color para la camiseta
1				
2				
3				
4				

Nombre _____   Hora _____

Fecha _____

AUDIO

Actividad 8

Your friend is babysitting for a family with an eight-year-old boy and a ten-year-old girl. Since they are a Spanish-speaking family, your friend wants you to go with her in case she doesn't understand everything that the mother tells her. Listen to the conversation to learn all the ground rules. Write either **sí** or **no** in each column that matches what the mother says that the boy or girl can do. Be sure to write **no** in both columns if neither is allowed to do it. Write **sí** in both columns if both are allowed to do it. You will hear this conversation twice.

AUDIO

Actividad 9

Look at the pictures in the chart below as you hear people describe their friends' bedrooms. Place a check in the chart that corresponds to all of the items mentioned by the friend. You will hear each set of statements twice.

	Javier	Sara	María	Marcos

Realidades 1

Capítulo 6A

Nombre _____

Fecha _____

Hora _____

WRITING

Actividad 10

Answer the following questions about your bedroom in complete sentences. If you prefer, you may write about your ideal bedroom.

1. ¿Cuál es tu color favorito?

_____

2. ¿De qué color es tu dormitorio?

_____

3. ¿Tienes una alfombra en tu dormitorio? ¿De qué color es?

_____

4. ¿Tienes un despertador? ¿Cuándo usas tu despertador?

_____

_____

5. ¿Qué muebles (*furniture*) tienes en tu dormitorio?

_____

_____

6. ¿Qué cosas electrónicas tienes en tu dormitorio?

_____

7. ¿Prefieres los videos o los DVDs? ¿Cuántos tienes?

_____

8. ¿Cuántos discos compactos tienes?

_____

Actividad 11

A. Draw your bedroom or your ideal bedroom (including furniture, electronics, windows, books, decorations, and other possessions) in the space provided below.

 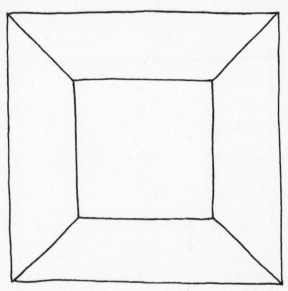

B. Now, compare the room that you drew with Juan's room on the left. Use the correct form of some of the following adjectives, or think of others: **práctico, interesante, grande, pequeño, mejor, peor, bonito, ordenado.**

| Modelo | *Mi dormitorio es menos interesante que el dormitorio de Juan.* |

1. _____

2. _____

3. _____

4. _____

5. _____

6. _____

Realidades ①

Capítulo 6A

Nombre _____

Hora _____

Fecha _____

WRITING

Actividad 12

You and your friends are comparing your English classes to determine which teacher's class to take next year. Read the information below, then compare the classes based on the criteria indicated. Follow the model.

	Clase A	Clase B	Clase C
Hora	Primera	Tercera	Octava
Profesor(a)	Profesora Brown — interesante	Profesor Martí — aburrido	Profesor Nicólas — muy interesante
Número de estudiantes	25	20	22
Dificultad	Difícil	Muy difícil	Fácil
Libros	Muy buenos	Aburridos	Buenos
Opinión general	A	B–	A–

Modelo Profesor *El profesor Martí es el menos interesante de los tres profesores.*

1. Hora (*temprano* or *tarde*)

   _____

2. Número de estudiantes (*grande* or *pequeña)*

   _____

3. Dificultad (*fácil* or *difícil*)

   _____

4. Libros (*buenos* or *malos*)

   _____

5. Opinión general (*mejor* or *peor*)

   _____

   _____

WRITING

Actividad 13

Your parents are hosting a family reunion, and nine extra people will be sleeping at your house. On the lines below, write where nine guests would sleep at your house. You may use your imagination if you prefer.

1. _____
   _____

2. _____
   _____

3. _____
   _____

4. _____
   _____

5. _____
   _____

6. _____
   _____

7. _____
   _____

8. _____
   _____

9. _____
   _____

Nombre _____   Hora _____

Fecha _____   **VIDEO**

Antes de ver el video

Actividad 1

Think of five chores you do at home. Then, write whether you like or don't like doing them using **me gusta** and **no me gusta nada**. Follow the model.

Modelo   *No me gusta nada limpiar mi dormitorio.* _____

1. _____

2. _____

3. _____

4. _____

5. _____

¿Comprendes?

Actividad 2

As you know from the video, Jorgito does all of the chores even though some were Elena's responsibility. Next to each chore listed below, tell whether it was Elena's responsibility or Jorgito's responsibility by writing the appropriate name in the space provided.

1. _____ quitar el polvo

2. _____ poner la mesa del comedor

3. _____ lavar los platos en la cocina

4. _____ hacer la cama en el dormitorio de Jorge

5. _____ hacer la cama en el cuarto de Elena

6. _____ arreglar el dormitorio de Jorge

7. _____ pasar la aspiradora

8. _____ dar de comer al perro

Actividad 3

Use the stills below from the video to help you answer the questions. Use complete sentences.

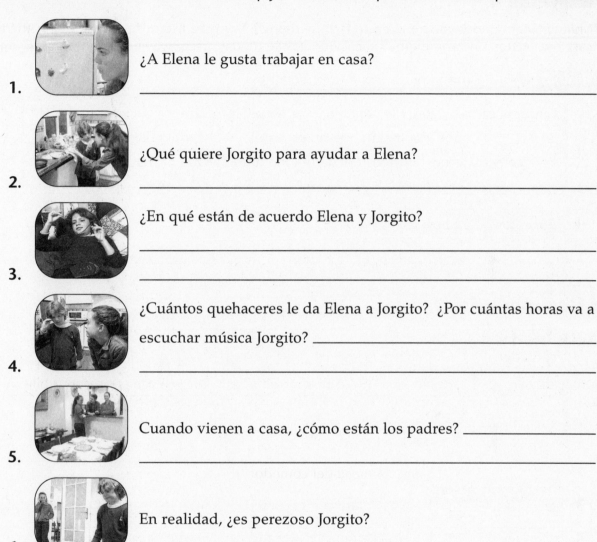

1. ¿A Elena le gusta trabajar en casa?
_____

2. ¿Qué quiere Jorgito para ayudar a Elena?
_____

3. ¿En qué están de acuerdo Elena y Jorgito?
_____
_____

4. ¿Cuántos quehaceres le da Elena a Jorgito? ¿Por cuántas horas va a escuchar música Jorgito? _____
_____

5. Cuando vienen a casa, ¿cómo están los padres? _____
_____

6. En realidad, ¿es perezoso Jorgito?
_____

Y, ¿qué más?

Actividad 4

What activities might you do in each of these rooms? From the list in the box below, name at least two things that you might logically do in each room. Each activity should be used only once.

hacer la cama   pasar la aspiradora   escuchar música   cocinar la comida   poner la mesa   lavar los platos   quitar el polvo   comer la cena   arreglar el dormitorio desordenado   hacer la tarea

1. dormitorio de Elena

_____   _____

2. sala

_____   _____

3. comedor

_____   _____

4. cocina

_____   _____

5. dormitorio de Jorge

_____   _____

Realidades 1

Capítulo 6B

Nombre _____

Fecha _____

Hora _____

AUDIO

Actividad 5

Listen as people look for things they have misplaced somewhere in their house. After each conversation, complete the sentence that explains what each person is looking for (**busca**) and in which room it is found. You will hear each dialogue twice.

1. La muchacha busca _____.

   Está en _____.

2. El muchacho busca _____.

   Está en _____.

3. La mujer busca _____.

   Está en _____.

4. El muchacho busca _____.

   Está en _____.

5. La muchacha busca _____.

   Está en _____.

Actividad 6

Señor Morales's nephew, Paco, volunteers to help his uncle move into a new apartment. However, Señor Morales is very distracted as he tells Paco where to put different things. Listen as he gives his nephew instructions and record in the grid below whether you think what he tells him to do each time is **lógico** (*logical*) **o ilógico** (*illogical*). You will hear each dialogue twice.

	1	2	3	4	5	6	7	8	9	10
lógico										
ilógico										

Actividad 7

Nico's parents are shocked when they come home from a trip to find that he hasn't done any of the chores that he promised to do. As they tell Nico what he needs to do, fill in the blanks below each picture with the corresponding number. You will hear each set of statements twice.

Actividad 8

Listen as each person rings a friend's doorbell and is told by the person who answers the door what the friend is doing at the moment. Based on that information, in which room of the house would you find the friend? As you listen to the conversations, look at the drawing of the house and write the number of the room that you think each friend might be in. You will hear each dialogue twice.

1. _____

2. _____

3. _____

4. _____

5. _____

6. _____

Realidades ❶

Capítulo 6B

Nombre _____

Fecha _____

Hora _____

AUDIO

Actividad 9

Some people always seem to get out of doing their chores at home. Listen as a few teens tell their parents why they should not or cannot do what their parents have asked them to do. As you listen, write in the chart below what the parent requests, such as **lavar los platos**. Then write in the teens' excuses, such as **está lavando el coche**. You will hear each conversation twice.

	Los quehaceres	Las excusas
Marcos		
Luis		
Marisol		
Jorge		
Elisa		

WRITING

Actividad 10

The Justino family is getting ready for their houseguests to arrive. Help Sra. Justino write the family's to-do list. Follow the model.

Modelo

En el dormitorio, tenemos que quitar el polvo, arreglar el cuarto y pasar la aspiradora.

1. _____

2. _____

3. _____

4. _____

WRITING

Actividad 11

The Boteros's son is going to stay with his grandmother in Puerto Rico for a month. His parents want to make sure that he is well-behaved and helps out around the house. Write ten commands the Boteros might give to their son. Follow the model.

Modelo	*Ayuda en la cocina, hijo.* _____

1. _____

2. _____

3. _____

4. _____

5. _____

6. _____

7. _____

8. _____

9. _____

10. _____

Realidades ❶

Capítulo 6B

Nombre

Fecha

Hora

WRITING

Actividad 12

The Galgo family is very busy on Sunday. Look at their schedule below and write what each family member is doing at the time given. Use your imagination, and use the model to help you.

	10:00	12:00	3:00	8:00
La Señora Galgo	hacer ejercicio	almorzar	trabajar	dormir
El Señor Galgo	trabajar	cortar el césped	preparar la cena	jugar al tenis
Rodrigo	arreglar el cuarto	comer	tocar la guitarra	estudiar
Mariana	nadar	poner la mesa	leer	ver la tele

Modelo 12:00 *A las doce, la Sra. Galgo está almorzando con sus amigos y el Sr. Galgo está cortando el césped. Rodrigo está comiendo una manzana y Mariana está poniendo la mesa.*

1. 10:00

_____

_____

_____

_____

2. 3:00

_____

_____

_____

_____

3. 8:00

_____

_____

_____

_____

Actividad 13

A. Read the letter that Marta wrote to "Querida Adela," an advice column in the local paper, because she was frustrated with having to help around the house.

> *Querida Adela:*
>
>   *Yo soy una hija de 16 años y no tengo tiempo para ayudar en la casa. Mis padres no comprenden que yo tengo mi propia vida y que mis amigos son más importantes que los quehaceres de la casa. ¿Qué debo hacer?*
>
>   *–Hija Malcontenta*

B. Now, imagine that you are Adela and are writing a response to Marta. In the first paragraph, tell her what she must do around the house. In the second, tell her what she can do to still have fun with her friends. Use the sentences already below to help you.

Querida Hija Malcontenta:

    Es verdad que tú tienes un problema. Piensas que tu vida con tus amigos es más

importante que tu vida con tu familia. Pero, hija, tú tienes responsabilidades.

Arregla tu cuarto. _____

_____

_____

_____

Tienes que ser una buena hija.

    Después de ayudar a tus padres, llama a tus amigos por teléfono.

_____

_____

_____. Tus padres van a estar más con-

tentos y tú vas a tener una vida mejor.

                                Buena suerte

                                Adela

Realidades ⓵

Capítulo 7A

Nombre _____

Fecha _____

Hora _____

VIDEO

Antes de ver el video

Actividad 1

In the next video, Claudia and Teresa go shopping for clothes. In order to make decisions on what they want they will sometimes make comparisons. Using the following words, make a comparative statement for each set. Follow the model.

Modelo   blusa roja / blusa amarilla

La blusa roja es más bonita que la blusa amarilla.

1. botas marrones / botas negras

_____

2. una falda larga / una mini falda

_____

3. un traje nuevo / un traje de moda (*in fashion*)

_____

4. Claudia – 16 años / Teresa – 15 años

_____

5. suéter que cuesta 40 dólares / suéter que cuesta 30 dólares

_____

¿Comprendes?

Actividad 2

Identify the speaker of the following quotes by writing the name of each person on the space provided.

1. "Tienes ropa muy bonita."   _____

2. "Quiero comprar algo nuevo."   _____

3. "¿Qué tal esta tienda?"   _____

Realidades 1

Capítulo 7A

Nombre _____

Fecha _____

Hora _____

VIDEO

4. "Pues entonces, ¿esta falda y esta blusa?" _____

5. "Busco algo bonito para una fiesta." _____

6. "Bueno, hay cosas que no cuestan tanto." _____

7. "Bueno, uhm, aquí en México no llevamos
esa ropa en las fiestas." _____

8. "¡... pero es mi gorra favorita!" _____

Actividad 3

Can you remember what happened in the video? Write the letter of the correct answer on the line.

1. A Teresa no le gusta la falda y el vestido; _____

   a. le quedan bien.

   b. le quedan más o menos.

   c. le quedan mal.

2. A Teresa no le gusta su ropa, pero sí tiene ropa _____

   a. bonita.

   b. fea.

   c. muy vieja.

3. Teresa quiere _____

   a. comprar algo extravagante.

   b. comprar algo nuevo.

   c. no ir a la fiesta.

Realidades ①

Capítulo 7A

Nombre _____

Fecha _____

Hora _____

VIDEO

4. Claudia quiere ver _____

   a. cuánto cuestan la falda y la blusa.

   b. si le quedan bien los jeans y la camiseta.

   c. otras cosas más bonitas.

5. Por fin las chicas deciden comprar _____

   a. unos jeans de cuatrocientos pesos con una camiseta de doscientos pesos.

   b. en otra tienda.

   c. una falda de trescientos pesos y un suéter de doscientos pesos.

Y, ¿qué más?

Actividad 4

Do you like the clothes that you have in your closet? Write one sentence about something in your closet that you do like, and why. Then write one sentence about something in your closet that you don't like, and why not. Follow the models.

Modelo 1 *Me gusta el suéter negro porque es bonito y puedo llevarlo*

cuando hace frío. _____

_____

_____

Modelo 2 *No me gustan los pantalones rojos porque son feos y me quedan mal.*

_____

_____

Realidades ①

Capítulo 7A

Nombre _____

Hora _____

Fecha _____

AUDIO

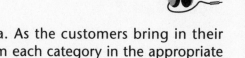

Actividad 5

Isabel is working at a laundry (**lavandería**) in Salamanca. As the customers bring in their order, write how many clothing items each person has from each category in the appropriate boxes. Then total the order and write the amount in the blanks provided in the grid for each customer. You will hear each dialogue twice.

LAVANDERÍA DOS PASOS

(Note: € is the symbol for Euros)

	Precios	Cliente 1	Cliente 2	Cliente 3	Cliente 4	Cliente 5
Blusas	3 €					
Vestidos	6 €					
Pantalones	8 €					
Faldas	5 €					
Suéteres	5 €					
Camisas	3 €					
Jeans	7 €					
Chaquetas	9 €					
Camisetas	3 €					
	TOTAL					

Actividad 6

Listen to the following items available from one of the shopping services on TV. You might not understand all of the words, but listen for the words that you do know in order to identify which item is being discussed. Then write down the price underneath the correct picture. You will hear each set of statements twice.

_____ _____ _____ _____ _____

Realidades ❶

Capítulo 7A

Nombre _____

Hora _____

Fecha _____

AUDIO

Actividad 7

Listen as friends talk about their plans for the weekend. Where are they thinking about going? What are they thinking about doing? How are they planning to dress? As you listen for these details, fill in the chart. You will hear each dialogue twice.

	¿Adónde piensa ir?	¿Qué piensa hacer?	¿Qué piensa llevar?
1. Paco			
2. Anita			
3. Ernesto			
4. Kiki			

Actividad 8

Susi is spending the summer in Ecuador, where she is living with a wonderful host family. As the summer comes to a close, she is searching for the perfect thank-you gifts for each member of the family. Listen as she talks to the sales clerk. In the chart below, write in the item that she decides to buy for each person in her new "family." You will hear this conversation twice.

Para la madre	Para el padre	Para el hijo, Luis	Para la hija, Marisol	Para el bebé

Actividad 9

What you wear can reveal secrets about your personality. Find out what type of message you send when you wear your favorite clothes and your favorite colors. As you listen to the descriptions, write down at least one word or phrase for each color personality and at least one article of clothing favored by that person. You will hear each set of statements twice.

EL COLOR	LA ROPA	LA PERSONALIDAD
Rojo		
Amarillo		
Morado		
Azul		
Anaranjado		
Marrón		
Gris		
Verde		
Negro		

Realidades ①

Capítulo 7A

Nombre _____

Fecha _____

Hora _____

WRITING

Actividad 10

Answer the following questions about clothing and shopping in complete sentences.

1. ¿Quién va mucho de compras en tu familia?

   _____

2. ¿Piensas comprar ropa nueva esta estación? ¿Qué piensas comprar?

   _____

   _____

3. ¿Cuál prefieres, la ropa del verano o la ropa del invierno? ¿Por qué?

   _____

   _____

4. ¿Prefieres la ropa de tus amigos o la ropa de tus padres? ¿Por qué?

   _____

   _____

5. ¿Prefieres llevar ropa formal o informal?

   _____

6. ¿Qué llevas normalmente para ir a la escuela?

   _____

   _____

   _____

7. ¿Cuál es tu ropa favorita? Describe.

   _____

   _____

   _____

Actividad 11

Some students are thinking about what to wear for the next school dance. Look at the pictures, then write complete sentences telling what the students might be thinking. Use the verbs **pensar, querer,** or **preferir.** Follow the model.

Modelo

María piensa llevar un vestido negro al baile. También quiere llevar unos zapatos negros. Quiere ser muy elegante.

1. _____

_____

_____

2. _____

_____

_____

3. _____

_____

_____

Realidades 1

Capítulo 7A

Nombre _____

Fecha _____

Hora _____

WRITING

Actividad 12

Pedro works in a department store and handles customer inquiries in the clearance clothing department. The items in his department are on sale, while the items in the rest of the store are full price. Help him answer customers' questions about the merchandise by writing complete sentences that include demonstrative adjectives. Follow the model.

Modelo   ¿Cuánto cuestan los suéteres?

Estos suéteres aquí cuestan cuarenta dólares y esos allí cuestan sesenta.

1. ¿Cuánto cuesta una gorra negra?

_____

2. ¿Cuánto cuestan los pantalones?

_____

3. ¿Las camisas cuestan diez dólares?

_____

4. ¿Cuánto cuesta un traje de baño?

_____

5. ¿Los jeans cuestan mucho?

_____

6. ¿La sudadera azul cuesta veinte dólares?

_____

7. ¿Cuánto cuestan las botas aquí?

_____

8. ¿Los abrigos cuestan mucho?

_____

Realidades ①

Capítulo 7A

Nombre _____

Fecha _____

Hora _____

WRITING

Actividad 13

You get a discount at the clothing store where you work after school, so you are going to buy presents for your friends and family there. Write complete sentences telling who you will buy gifts for and why you will choose each person's gift. Use the model to help you.

Modelo   *Pienso comprar este suéter azul para mi madre porque ella prefiere la ropa del invierno.*

1. _____

_____

2. _____

_____

3. _____

_____

4. _____

_____

5. _____

_____

Realidades ①

Capítulo 7B

Nombre _____

Hora _____

Fecha _____

VIDEO

Antes de ver el video

Actividad 1

Where do you like to shop? With a partner, write three things you like to buy and the best place to buy them.

Cosas para comprar

_____

_____

_____

Lugares donde comprarlas

_____

_____

_____

¿Comprendes?

Actividad 2

In the video, Claudia and Manolo go many places to find a gift for Manolo's aunt. Look at the places from the video below and number them in the order in which Manolo and Claudia pass them (from beginning to end).

_____ el almacén

_____ la joyería

_____ la tienda de software

_____ la parada de autobuses

_____ el centro comercial

Actividad 3

What happens when Claudia helps Manolo shop? Circle the letter of the correct answers.

1. Manolo necesita comprar un regalo para su tía porque
   a. mañana es su cumpleaños.
   b. mañana es su aniversario de bodas.
   c. mañana es su quinceañera.

2. El año pasado Manolo le compró a su tía
   a. unos aretes en la joyería.
   b. un libro en una librería.
   c. una corbata muy barata.

3. En el centro comercial, ellos ven
   a. videojuegos y software.
   b. pocas cosas en descuento.
   c. anteojos para sol, bolsos, carteras y llaveros.

4. Por fin, deciden comprar para la tía
   a. una cartera.
   b. un collar.
   c. un anillo.

5. Hay una confusión y Manolo le regala a la tía
   a. una pulsera.
   b. unos guantes.
   c. un collar de perro.

Realidades 1

Capítulo 7B

Nombre _____

Hora _____

Fecha _____

VIDEO

Y, ¿qué más?

Actividad 4

You are shopping for a birthday gift for your mother. Fill in the dialogue below with your possible responses.

DEPENDIENTE: ¿Qué desea usted?

TÚ: _____

_____

DEPENDIENTE: ¿Prefiere ver ropa, perfumes o joyas para ella?

TÚ: _____

_____

DEPENDIENTE: Aquí hay muchos artículos, pero no cuestan tanto.

TÚ: _____

_____

Actividad 5

Sometimes giving gifts is even more fun than receiving them! Listen as people talk about gifts they enjoy giving to their friends and family. Match the pictures below with the corresponding description you hear. Then, in the spaces next to each gift, write where the person bought the gift and what the person paid for it. You will hear each set of statements twice.

	Descripción	Lugar de compra	Precio
1.	_____	_____	_____
2.	_____	_____	_____
3.	_____	_____	_____
4.	_____	_____	_____
5.	_____	_____	_____

Actividad 6

Listen to the following mini-conversations about different kinds of stores. Circle **lógico** if the conversation makes sense and **ilógico** if it does not. You will hear each dialogue twice.

1. lógico	ilógico		**6.** lógico	ilógico
2. lógico	ilógico		**7.** lógico	ilógico
3. lógico	ilógico		**8.** lógico	ilógico
4. lógico	ilógico		**9.** lógico	ilógico
5. lógico	ilógico		**10.** lógico	ilógico

Actividad 7

Listen as Lorena shows a friend her photographs. Write a sentence describing each one as you hear Lorena describe it. You will hear each conversation twice.

1. Lorena _____ hace _____.

2. Lorena _____ hace _____.

3. Lorena _____ hace _____.

4. Lorena _____ hace _____.

5. Lorena _____ hace _____.

Actividad 8

You have been waiting in line all day at the mall, so you have overheard many conversations as you waited. See if you can match each conversation with the illustrations below and write the number of each conversation under the correct illustration. You will hear each conversation twice.

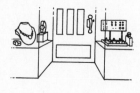   

_____ _____ _____ _____

Realidades ①

Capítulo 7B

Nombre _____

Hora _____

Fecha _____

AUDIO

Actividad 9

As a special holiday service, **El Almacén Continental** is sponsoring a hotline that customers can call to get gift ideas. Listen as callers tell the store specialist what they have bought for a particular person in the past. Then listen to the specialist's suggestion for this year's gift. Use the chart below to take notes. You will hear each conversation twice.

	La personalidad y las actividades de la persona	El regalo del año pasado	¿Un regalo para este año?
1			
2			
3			
4			
5			

Realidades ①

Capítulo 7B

Nombre _____

Fecha _____

Hora _____

WRITING

Actividad 10

You are talking to a friend about what you buy when you go shopping. Tell what items you usually buy in each of the specialty shops suggested by the pictures. Then, tell what other items are available at the store. Use the model to help you.

Modelo

En la zapatería, compro zapatos y botas. También es posible comprar guantes y carteras en una zapatería.

1. _____

_____

_____

_____

2. _____

_____

_____

_____

3. _____

_____

_____

_____

Nombre _____   Hora _____

Fecha _____

WRITING

Actividad 11

In your Spanish class, you are asked to learn the dates of some important events in the history and culture of Spanish-speaking countries. To help you memorize these dates, write sentences telling when each event occurred. Follow the model.

Modelo   Pablo Picasso / pintar su cuadro *Guernica* / 1937

Pablo Picasso pintó su cuadro Guernica en 1937.

1. Los Estados Unidos / declarar su independencia / el cuatro de julio, 1776

   _____

2. Vicente Fox / ganar la presidencia de México / 2000

   _____

3. Antonio Banderas / actuar en la película *The Mambo Kings* / 1993

   _____

4. Los jugadores argentinos / ganar la Copa Mundial (*World Cup*) / 1986

   _____

5. Yo / comprar mis primeros zapatos / ???

   _____

6. Nosotros / entrar en la clase de español / ???

   _____

7. Los Juegos Olímpicos / pasar en España / 1992

   _____

8. México / declarar su independencia / el quince de septiembre, 1810

   _____

9. Simón Bolívar / liberar a Venezuela / 1821

   _____

Realidades 1

Capítulo 7B

Nombre _____

Hora _____

Fecha _____

WRITING

Actividad 12

The people in your neighborhood were very busy yesterday. Write at least three sentences about what they all did based on the pictures, using at least one of these verbs: **buscar, jugar, pagar, practicar, sacar, tocar.** Follow the model.

Modelo   El Sr. Rodríguez

Ayer el Sr. Rodríguez enseñó la clase de español. La clase practicó la lección. Los estudiantes usaron las computadoras para hacer las actividades.

1.   Andrés

_____

_____

_____

2.   yo

_____

_____

_____

3.   yo   mi madre

_____

_____

_____

Realidades ❶

Capítulo 7B

Nombre _____

Hora _____

Fecha _____

WRITING

4. tú

_____

_____

_____

5. Juana e Inés

_____

_____

_____

Actividad 13

You are writing a letter to your aunt in Mexico to tell her what you bought for your family for the holidays. In the letter, tell what you bought for each person, in what stores you found the items, and how much you paid. The letter has been started for you.

Querida Tía:

    Saludos de los Estados Unidos. Te escribo para decirte que terminé de comprar los

regalos para la familia. Para _____ , compré un suéter bonito. ¡Lo encontré en

el almacén por sólo veinte dólares! _____

_____

_____

_____

_____

    Bueno, nos vemos en una semana. ¡Buena suerte con las compras!

                           Un fuerte abrazo,

                           Tu sobrino(a) _____

Nombre _____   Hora _____

Fecha _____

VIDEO

Antes de ver el video

Actividad 1

You can see and learn a lot on a day trip. Make a list of four places you would like to visit for the day, and write next to each one the main attraction that you would like to see there. Follow the model.

Lugares	Cosas que ver
Modelo *Granada, España*	*La Alhambra*
_____	_____
_____	_____
_____	_____

¿Comprendes?

Actividad 2

Raúl, Gloria, and Tomás went on a day trip to San José and Sarapiquí Park. Under each heading, write the things that they saw in San José and the things that they saw in Sarapiquí Park.

Ministerio de Cultura	mono	Parque España	Catarata La Paz
Gran Terminal del Caribe	palma	bosque lluvioso	Teatro Nacional

San José	Parque Sarapiquí
_____	_____
_____	_____
_____	_____

Actividad 3

Based on the video story that you just watched, circle the most appropriate word to complete each statement.

1. Raúl, Gloria y Tomás salieron de la casa muy (tarde / temprano) para ir al parque Sarapiquí.

2. Para ir al parque ellos tomaron el (autobús / avión).

3. El viaje dura (una hora y media / dos horas), porque el parque está a 82 (kilómetros / millas) de San José.

4. En el parque (hace mucho calor / no hace ni frío ni calor) pero llueve mucho.

5. Raúl compra los (libros / boletos) en la Estación Biológica La Selva y cuestan 3,600 (pesos / colones).

6. Tomás tiene la (mochila / cámara) y el (boleto / mapa) y está listo para explorar el parque.

7. Ellos tienen mucho cuidado cuando caminan, pues las raíces de los árboles son muy (grandes / interesantes).

8. Gloria le dice a Tomás: "Hay más de cuatrocientas especies de (monos / aves) en el parque."

9. Ellos tienen problemas al (sacar las fotos / regresar a casa). Pero Tomás (quiere / no quiere) continuar.

10. Raúl dice: "Fue un día (interesante / desastre) pero un poco (difícil / aburrido) para Tomás."

Nombre _____

Hora _____

Fecha _____

VIDEO

Y, ¿qué más?

Actividad 4

Based on what you learned in the video, imagine that you took a field trip to Costa Rica. Your best friend is curious about your trip. Answer your friend's questions below.

1. —¿Cómo es el parque Sarapiquí?

— _____

2. —¿Sacaste fotos del parque?

— _____

3. —¿Qué fue lo que más te gustó?

— _____

4. —¿Qué fue lo que menos te gustó?

— _____

5. —¿Cuál es la comida típica de Costa Rica?

— _____

Realidades 1

Capítulo 8A

Nombre _____

Fecha _____

Hora _____

AUDIO

Actividad 5

You call a toll-free telephone number in order to qualify for the popular radio game show, **"Palabras Secretas"** (*Secret Words*). Your challenge is to guess each secret word within ten seconds. Listen to the clues and try to guess the word as the clock is ticking. You must write your answer down before the buzzer in order to be ready for the next one. You will hear each set of statements twice.

1. _____   5. _____

2. _____   6. _____

3. _____   7. _____

4. _____   8. _____

Actividad 6

Listen as a husband and wife talk to a travel agent about their upcoming vacation. Where would each like to go? What type of things would each like to do? Most importantly, do they agree on what is the ideal trip? As you listen, write as much information as you can in each person's travel profile in the chart below. Can you think of a place they could go where both of them would be happy? You will hear this conversation twice.

	EL SEÑOR	LA SEÑORA
¿Adónde le gustaría ir?		
¿Por qué le gustaría ir a ese lugar?		
Cuando va de vacaciones, ¿qué le gustaría hacer?	1. 2.	1. 2.
¿Qué le gustaría ver?	1. 2.	1. 2.
¿Cómo le gustaría viajar?		
¿Adónde deben ir?		

Actividad 7

Listen as mothers call their teenaged sons and daughters on their cell phones to see if they have done what they were asked to do. Based on what each teenager says, categorize the answers in the chart. You will hear each conversation twice.

	1	2	3	4	5	6	7	8	9	10
Teen did what the parent asked him or her to do.										
Teen is in the middle of doing what the parent asked him or her to do.										
Teen says he/she is going to do what the parent asked him/her to do.										

Actividad 8

Your Spanish teacher has asked the students in your class to survey each other about a topic of interest. In order to give you a model to follow, your teacher will play a recording of part of a student's survey from last year. Listen to the student's questions, and fill in his survey form. You will hear each conversation twice.

	¿EL LUGAR?
1. Marco	
2. Patricia	
3. Chucho	
4. Rita	
5. Margarita	

Actividad 9

Everyone loves a superhero, and the listeners of this Hispanic radio station are no exception. Listen to today's episode of "Super Tigre," as the hero helps his friends try to locate the evil Rona Robles! Super Tigre tracks Rona Robles down by asking people when they last saw her and where she went. Keep track of what the people said by filling in the chart. You will hear each conversation twice.

	¿Dónde la vio?	¿A qué hora la vio?	¿Qué hizo ella? *(What did she do?)*	¿Adónde fue ella?
1				
2				
3				
4				
5				

Where did Super Tigre finally find Rona Robles? _____

Realidades 1

Capítulo 8A

Nombre _____

Hora _____

Fecha _____

WRITING

Actividad 10

Answer the following questions in complete sentences.

1. ¿Te gusta ir de viaje? ¿Te gustaría más ir de vacaciones al campo o a una ciudad?

   _____

   _____

2. ¿Visitaste algún parque nacional en el pasado? ¿Cuál(es)? Si no, ¿te gustaría visitar

   un parque nacional? _____

   _____

3. ¿Vives cerca de un lago? ¿Cómo se llama? ¿Te gusta nadar? ¿Pasear en bote?

   _____

   _____

4. ¿Te gusta ir al mar? ¿Qué te gusta hacer allí? Si no, ¿por qué no? _____

   _____

   _____

5. ¿Montaste a caballo alguna vez? ¿Te gustó o no? Si no, ¿te gustaría montar a caballo?

   _____

   _____

6. Describe tu lugar favorito para vivir. ¿Está cerca de un lago? ¿Cerca o lejos de
   la ciudad? ¿Hay montañas / museos / parques / un mar cerca de tu casa ideal?

   _____

   _____

   _____

Nombre _____ Hora _____

Fecha _____

Actividad 11

You and your friends are talking about what you did over the weekend. Write complete sentences based on the illustrations to tell what the following people did. Follow the model.

Modelo   Pablo *vio una película* _____.

1.   Mariela y su madre _____.

2.   Nosotros _____.

3.   Yo _____.

4.   Roberto _____.

5.   Norma _____.

6.   Tú _____.

7.   Ignacio e Isabel _____.

Realidades ①

Capítulo 8A

Nombre _____

Hora _____

Fecha _____

WRITING

Actividad 12

You and your friends were very busy yesterday. Tell all the places where each person went using the illustrations as clues. Follow the model.

Modelo

Melisa y su padre _fueron de compras._
Después, fueron al cine.

1. David _____

   _____

   _____

2. Yo _____

   _____

   _____

3. Nosotros _____

   _____

   _____

4. Raquel y Tito _____

   _____

   _____

Realidades 1

Capítulo 8A

Nombre _____

Hora _____

Fecha _____

WRITING

Actividad 13

A. Write two sentences telling what places you visited the last time you went on vacation. You can write about your ideal vacation if you would prefer. Follow the model.

Modelo *Fui al parque de diversiones.* _____

1. _____

2. _____

B. Write two sentences telling about people you saw when you were on vacation.

Modelo *Vi a mi abuela.* _____

1. _____

2. _____

C. Now, complete the letter below to your friend. Use your sentences from Part A and Part B and additional details to tell him or her about your vacation.

Querido(a) _____ :

　　¡Hola! ¿Cómo estás? Gracias por tu carta de la semana pasada. Te voy a contar un poco de nuestras vacaciones del mes pasado. _____

_____

_____

_____

Y cuando fuimos a otro lugar, vimos _____

_____

_____

_____

_____

Un abrazo,

_____

Realidades 1

Capítulo 8B

Nombre _____

Hora _____

Fecha _____

VIDEO

Antes de ver el video

Actividad 1

There are lots of things you can do to make the world a better place. Under each category, write two things that you would like to do to help.

Cómo ayudar...

en mi comunidad _____

_____

con el ambiente _____

_____

¿Comprendes?

Actividad 2

In the video, the friends talk about how to help in their communities through volunteer work. Circle the letter of the appropriate answer for each question.

1. Gloria y Raúl trabajan como voluntarios en

    a. un centro de ancianos.

    b. Casa Latina.

    c. el Hospital Nacional de Niños.

2. Tomás va al hospital porque

    a. está enfermo.

    b. a él le encanta el trabajo voluntario.

    c. tiene que llevar ropa para los niños.

3. Gloria dice: "Trabajar con los niños en el hospital es

    a. muy aburrido."

    b. una experiencia inolvidable."

    c. un trabajo que no me gusta."

Realidades ❶

Capítulo 8B

Nombre _____

Hora _____

Fecha _____

VIDEO

4. En su comunidad, Tomás trabaja como voluntario

   a. dando comida a los pobres.

   b. enseñando a leer a los ancianos.

   c. recogiendo ropa usada para los pobres.

5. Ellos también cuidan el ambiente reciclando

   a. aluminio y periódicos.

   b. papel, plástico y vidrio.

   c. papel, vidrio y aluminio.

Actividad 3

Fill in the blanks from the box below to complete the story.

reciclar	importante	libros	pasado
ancianos	comunidad	voluntarios	difícil
lava	simpáticos	trabajo	

En el Hospital Nacional de Niños, Tomás y Gloria trabajan como (1) _____ .

Allí ellos cantan, leen (2) _____ y juegan con los niños. A veces los niños

están muy enfermos y es (3) _____ , pero los niños son muy

(4) _____ . Raúl trabajó en un centro de (5) _____ el año (6)

_____ . Allí les ayudó con la comida y hablando con ellos.

   Tomás también trabaja en su (7) _____ ; él ayuda a recoger ropa usada.

Después la separa, la (8) _____ y luego la da a la gente pobre del barrio.

Es mucho (9) _____ , pero le gusta.

   Todos ellos ayudan a (10) _____ el papel y las botellas pues, piensan que

reciclar y conservar es muy (11) _____ .

Realidades 1

Capítulo 8B

Nombre _____

Hora _____

Fecha _____

VIDEO

Y, ¿qué más?

Actividad 4

Now that you have seen Tomás, Gloria, and Raúl working in various ways to help others, think about the organizations that make it possible for them to do this work. Imagine that you work with one of the organizations listed below, and write a paragraph about your experiences. Use the model to help you.

el Hospital Nacional de Niños

un centro de ancianos

el club Casa Latina

Modelo   *Me gusta trabajar en el centro de ancianos. Les ayudo con la*
         comida y paso tiempo escuchando sus cuentos.

_____

_____

_____

_____

_____

_____

Realidades ❶

Capítulo 8B

Nombre _____

Hora _____

Fecha _____

AUDIO

Actividad 5

Listen as Sra. Muñoz, the Spanish Club sponsor, asks several students what they did last weekend. If a student's actions had a positive impact on their community, place a check mark in the corresponding box or boxes. If a student's actions had no positive effect on their community, place an *X* in the corresponding box or boxes. You will hear each conversation twice.

	Javier	Ana	José	Celi	Pablo	Laura	Sra. Muñoz
enseñar a los niños a leer							
reciclar la basura de las calles							
jugar al fútbol con amigos							
recoger y lavar la ropa usada para la gente pobre							
trabajar en un centro para ancianos							
traer juguetes a los niños que están en el hospital							
trabajar en un restaurante del centro comercial							

Actividad 6

Listen as people talk about what they did last Saturday. Did they do volunteer work in the community or did they earn spending money for themselves? Place a check mark in the correct box on the grid. You will hear each set of statements twice.

	1	2	3	4	5	6	7	8

Actividad 7

Listen as our leaders, friends, and family give advice to teenagers about what we must do to serve our communities. Use the grid below to take notes as you listen. Then, use your notes to complete the sentences below. For example, you might write **"El vicepresidente de los Estados Unidos *dice que hay que reciclar la basura de las calles*."** In the last sentence, complete a statement about your personal suggestion for others. You will hear each set of statements twice.

¿Quién(es) lo dice(n)?	¿Qué dice(n)?
1. El presidente de los Estados Unidos	
2. Mis padres	
3. Los médicos del hospital	
4. Mis profesores	
5. Mis amigos y yo	

1. El presidente de los Estados Unidos _____

_____ .

2. Los padres _____

_____ .

3. Los médicos _____

_____ .

4. Los profesores _____

_____ .

5. Mis amigos _____

_____ .

6. Yo _____

_____ .

Actividad 8

As you hear each of the following statements, imagine whom the speaker might be addressing. Choose from the list of people, and write the number of the statement on the corresponding blank. You will hear each set of statements twice.

_____ al médico   _____ a sus padres

_____ a la policía   _____ a un niño de cinco años

_____ al camarero   _____ a un voluntario del hospital

_____ a la profesora de español   _____ a una persona que trabaja en el zoológico

Actividad 9

Abuela Consuelo always has her grandchildren over for the holidays. She wants to know what they have done over the past year. They also remind her what she gave them last year as a gift. Use the grid to help keep track of each grandchild's story. You will hear each conversation twice.

	¿Qué hizo el niño el año pasado?	¿Qué le dio la abuela al niño el año pasado?
Marta		
Jorge		
Sara		
Miguel		
Angélica		

Realidades ❶

Capítulo 8B

Nombre _____

Fecha _____

Hora _____

WRITING

Actividad 10

Answer the following questions in complete sentences.

1. ¿Hay lugares para hacer trabajo voluntario en tu comunidad?

   _____

   ¿Qué hacen allí? _____

   _____

2. ¿Te gustaría trabajar como voluntario en:

   un hospital? ¿Por qué? _____

   _____

   un centro para personas pobres? ¿Por qué? _____

   _____

   un centro para ancianos? ¿Por qué? _____

   _____

3. ¿Tu familia recicla? _____

   ¿Qué reciclan Uds.? _____

   _____

   ¿Por qué es importante reciclar? _____

   _____

   ¿Te gustaría ayudar con el reciclaje en tu comunidad? _____

   _____

Actividad 11

All of the following people were asked to speak on a subject. You are reporting on what everyone says. Use each item only once. Follow the model.

yo	el trabajo voluntario
nosotros	el campamento de deportes
Sra. Ayala	el reciclaje
Dr. Riviera	el fútbol
tú	el teatro
Paco	la ropa
José y María	la salud
Alicia y yo	los quehaceres

Modelo _La señora Ayala dice que el trabajo voluntario es una_
experiencia inolvidable.

1. _____

2. _____

3. _____

4. _____

5. _____

6. _____

7. _____

Realidades ❶

Capítulo 8B

Nombre _____

Hora _____

Fecha _____

WRITING

Actividad 12

You are finding out what everyone's plans are for the weekend. Choose a verb and a direct object pronoun from the banks and write a sentence about weekend plans for each subject given. Use each verb only once. Follow the model.

ayudar	dar	decir	enseñar	escribir
hacer	invitar	leer	llevar	traer

me	te	le	nos	les

Modelo   *Miguel y Elena nos invitan a su fiesta.*

1. Mis padres _____.

2. Yo _____.

3. Uds. _____.

4. Nuestra profesora de español _____.

5. El presidente _____.

6. Rafael y Gabriel _____.

7. Tu mejor amigo _____.

8. El Sr. Fuentes _____.

9. La Sra. Allende _____.

10. Tú _____.

Actividad 13

Last week, your Spanish class did some volunteer work at the local nursing home. Read the thank you letter from the residents, then write a paragraph explaining at least four things that you and your classmates did for them. Remember to use the preterite tense and indirect object pronouns where necessary. Follow the model.

Queridos muchachos:

Les escribimos para decirles "gracias" por su generosa visita de la semana pasada. A la señora Blanco le gustó el libro de poesía que Uds. le regalaron. Todos lo pasamos bien. Nos gustó especialmente la canción "Feliz Navidad" que cantó Luisita. El señor Marcos todavía habla de los pasteles que las chicas le trajeron. Y nuestro jardín está más bonito que nunca, después de todo su trabajo. En fin, mil gracias de parte de todos aquí en Pinos Sombreados. Esperamos verles pronto.

Fuertes abrazos,

Los residentes

Modelo *Nosotros visitamos a los residentes de Pinos Sombreados la semana pasada.*

_____

_____

_____

_____

_____

_____

_____

_____

_____

Nombre _____   Hora _____

Fecha _____   **VIDEO**

Antes de ver el video

Actividad 1

In the second column, write the title of a movie or a television program that is associated with the category in the first column. The first one is done for you.

Programa o película	Nombre del programa o película
telenovelas	"Days of Our Lives"
noticias	
programas de entrevistas	
programas de la vida real	
películas de ciencia ficción	
programas de concurso	
programas educativos	
programas de deportes	
comedias	
dibujos animados	
películas románticas	
programas infantiles	

Realidades ❶

Capítulo 9A

Nombre _____

Fecha _____

Hora _____

VIDEO

¿Comprendes?

Actividad 2

Look at the pictures and write what type of program each one is. Then, write the name of the character in the video who likes this type of program.

	CATEGORY	CHARACTER'S NAME
1.	_____	_____
2.	_____	_____
3.	_____	_____
4.	_____	_____
5.	_____	_____

Actividad 3

Using complete sentences, answer the following questions about what happens in the video.

1. ¿Quién tiene el mando a distancia primero?

_____

2. ¿Qué piensa Ana de la telenovela "El amor es loco"?

_____

Realidades ①

Capítulo 9A

Nombre _____

Hora _____

Fecha _____

VIDEO

3. ¿A quiénes les encantan las telenovelas?

_____

4. ¿Qué piensa Ignacio de los programas de la vida real?

_____

5. ¿Qué piensa Jorgito de escuchar música en el cuarto de su hermana?

_____

6. ¿Qué deciden hacer los amigos al final?

_____

7. ¿Qué quiere ver Elena en el cine? ¿Están de acuerdo Ignacio y Javier?

_____

Y, ¿qué más?

Actividad 4

What kind of TV programs do you like? What type of movies do you enjoy watching? Explain your preferences. Follow the model.

Modelo

A mí me gustan mucho los programas de concursos; son muy divertidos porque puedes jugarlos en casa con tu familia o amigos. Mi hermano prefiere los deportes; siempre quiere el mando a distancia para ver los juegos. Cuando voy al cine prefiero ver comedias, pues las películas románticas son aburridas.

_____

_____

_____

_____

Realidades ❶

Capítulo 9A

Nombre _____

Fecha _____

Hora _____

AUDIO

Actividad 5

Your friend is reading you the television line-up for a local television station. After listening to each program description, fill in on the grid what day or days the program is shown, what time it is shown, and what type of program it is. You will hear each set of statements twice.

	Día(s)	Hora	Clase de programa
"Mi computadora"			
"La detective Morales"			
"Cine en su sofá"			
"Las aventuras del Gato Félix"			
"Cara a cara"			
"Lo mejor del béisbol"			
"Marisol"			
"Festival"			
"Treinta minutos"			
"Las Américas"			

Actividad 6

Listen as people in a video rental store talk about what kind of movie they want to rent. After listening to each conversation, put the letter of the type of film they agree on in the space provided. You will hear each conversation twice.

1. _____   A. una película policíaca

2. _____   B. una comedia

3. _____   C. un drama

4. _____   D. una película de ciencia ficción

5. _____   E. una película romántica

6. _____   F. una película de horror

7. _____   G. una película de dibujos animados

Realidades 1

Capítulo 9A

Nombre _____

Hora _____

Fecha _____

AUDIO

Actividad 7

Listen to a film critic interviewing five people on opening night of the movie *Marruecos*. After listening to each person's interview, circle the number of stars that closely matches the person's opinion of the movie, from a low rating of one star to a high rating of four. After noting all of the opinions, give the movie an overall rating of one to four stars, and give a reason for your answer. You will hear each conversation twice.

	No le gustó nada	Le gustó más o menos	Le gustó mucho	Le encantó
1.	[★]	[★★]	[★★★]	[★★★★]
2.	[★]	[★★]	[★★★]	[★★★★]
3.	[★]	[★★]	[★★★]	[★★★★]
4.	[★]	[★★]	[★★★]	[★★★★]
5.	[★]	[★★]	[★★★]	[★★★★]

¿Cuántas estrellas para *Marruecos*? ¿Por qué? _____

Actividad 8

Listen as two friends talk on the phone about what they just saw on TV. Do they seem to like the same type of programs? As you listen to their conversation, fill in the Venn diagram, indicating: 1) which programs only Alicia likes; 2) which programs both Alicia and Laura like; and 3) which programs only Laura likes. You will hear this conversation twice.

a Alicia   a ellos   a Laura

Actividad 9

Listen as a television critic reviews some of the new shows of the season. As you listen, determine which shows he likes and dislikes, and why. Fill in the chart. You will hear each paragraph twice.

	Le gusta...	¿Por qué le gusta?	No le gusta...	¿Por qué no le gusta?
1				
2				
3				
4				
5				

Actividad 10

Answer the following questions about movies and television.

1. ¿Te gusta ir al cine?

_____

2. ¿Prefieres los dramas o las comedias? ¿Por qué? _____

_____

_____

3. ¿Cómo se llama tu película favorita? ¿Qué clase de película es?

_____

_____

4. ¿Te gustan las películas policíacas? ¿Por qué? _____

_____

5. ¿Te gusta más ver la tele o leer? ¿Por qué? _____

_____

_____

6. ¿Qué clase de programas prefieres? ¿Por qué? _____

_____

_____

7. ¿Cuántos canales de televisión puedes ver en casa? _____

¿Cuál es tu canal favorito? _____

¿Por qué? _____

8. ¿Tienes un programa favorito? ¿Cómo se llama? _____

_____

Realidades **1**

Capítulo 9A

Nombre _____

Hora _____

Fecha _____

WRITING

Actividad 11

Your school newspaper printed a picture of the preparations for the Cinco de Mayo party at your school. Describe the photo using a form of **acabar de** + infinitive to tell what everyone just finished doing before the picture was taken.

Modelo *Horacio Ibáñez acaba de sacar la foto.* _____

1. Isabel _____

_____

2. Julia y Ramón _____

_____

3. Yo _____

_____

4. La señora Lemaños _____

_____

5. Ana _____

_____

Nombre _____ Hora _____

Fecha _____ **WRITING**

Actividad 12

You and your friends are talking about movies. Tell about people's preferences by choosing a subject from the first column and matching it with words from the other two columns to make complete sentences. Use each subject only once, but words from the other columns can be used more than once. Follow the model.

nosotros	gustar	las películas románticas
mis padres	encantar	las película de horror
mí	aburrir	las películas policíacas
ti	interesar	las comedias
los profesores	disgustar	los dramas
mis amigas		
mi abuelo		

Modelo *A mí me encantan las películas románticas.* _____

1. _____

2. _____

3. _____

4. _____

5. _____

6. _____

Nombre _____ Hora _____

Fecha _____

Actividad 13

You are writing your new Spanish-speaking pen pal an e-mail about American television. First tell him about a program that you just saw. What type of show was it? Did you like it? Was it interesting? Then, tell him about two other types of TV shows that are popular in America. Make sure to tell him your opinion of these types of shows, and what some other people you know think about them.

Fecha: 20 de abril

Tema: La televisión

Querido Pancho:

   ¡Hola! ¿Cómo estás? Acabo de terminar de ver el programa _____

_____ . A mí _____

_____

_____

_____

   En los Estados Unidos, la gente ve mucho la tele. _____

_____

_____

_____

_____

¡Te escribo pronto!

                                          Un abrazo,

                                          _____

Realidades ❶

Capítulo 9B

Nombre _____

Fecha _____

Hora _____

VIDEO

Antes de ver el video

Actividad 1

How do you communicate with your friends from far away? Using the word bank below, write two sentences about how you might stay in touch with long distance friends.

cámara digital	correo electrónico
ordenador / computadora	cibercafé
navegar en la Red	página Web
información	salones de chat
dirección electrónica	foto digital

_____

_____

_____

_____

¿Comprendes?

Actividad 2

Javier is becoming accustomed to living in Spain, but he has a lot to learn about technology. What does Ana teach him? Write **cierto** (*true*) or **falso** (*false*) next to each statement.

1. Javier conoce muy bien las cámaras digitales. _____

2. Él va a enviar una tarjeta a su amigo Esteban. _____

3. Javier le saca una foto de Ana y le gusta la cámara. _____

4. Él piensa que no es muy complicada la cámara digital. _____

5. Ana lo lleva a un cibercafé, para ordenar un café. _____

6. Empiezan a navegar en la Red. _____

7. Ana busca su página Web, pero Javier no la quiere ver. _____

8. No hay mucha información en la Red. _____

9. Pueden visitar los salones de chat, pero
prefieren escribirle un correo electrónico a Esteban. _____

10. Esteban ve la foto digital de su amigo y piensa que está triste. _____

Actividad 3

Complete the sentences below with information from the video.

1. Javier va a enviar _____ a su amigo Esteban.

2. Ana saca muchas fotos con su _____ .

3. A Javier le gusta la cámara de Ana porque no es muy _____ .

4. Ana y Javier van a un _____ para escribirle a Esteban por _____ electrónico.

5. Según Ana, el ordenador _____ para mucho.

6. Javier quiere saber qué tal fue el _____ de Cristina.

VIDEO

Y, ¿qué más?

Actividad 4

You heard Ana and Javier talk about the many ways they use computers. Write a paragraph describing your two favorite ways to use a computer. Use the model to give you an idea of how to start.

Modelo *En mi casa todos usan la computadora. Para mí el uso más importante es...*

_____

_____

_____

_____

_____

_____

Realidades ❶

Capítulo 9B

Nombre _____

Fecha _____

Hora _____

AUDIO

Actividad 5

While navigating a new Web site, two friends click on a link to a self-quiz to find out if they are **CiberAdictos.** Based on their discussion of each question, write in the chart below whether you think they answered **sí** or **no**. According to the Web site, a score of more than six **sí** answers determines that you are a **CiberAdicto.** You will hear each set of statements twice.

	1	2	3	4	5	6	7	8	¿Es CiberAdicto?
Rafael									
Miguel									

Actividad 6

Víctor has studied for the first quiz in his beginning technology class. As the teacher reads each statement, he is to answer **falso** or **cierto**. Listen to the statements and write the answers in the boxes, and take the quiz too. Would you be able to score 100%? You will hear each statement twice.

1	2	3	4	5	6	7	8	9	10

Actividad 7

Listen to the following conversations that you overhear while sitting at a table in the Café Mariposa. After listening to what each person is saying, write what they asked for in the first column and what they were served in the second column. You will hear each statement twice.

Persona	Comida pedida	Comida servida
1. Señor Cruz		
2. Señora Vargas		
3. Señor Ávila		
4. Marcelo y Daniele		
5. Señor Urbina		
6. Señora Campos		
7. Señora Suerte		

Realidades ❶

Capítulo 9B

Nombre _____

Fecha _____

Hora _____

AUDIO

Actividad 8

Listen as teenagers talk to each other about what they need to learn how to do. The second teenager is always able to suggest someone whom the first teenager should ask for help. Match the person who is suggested to the correct picture. You will hear each set of statements twice.

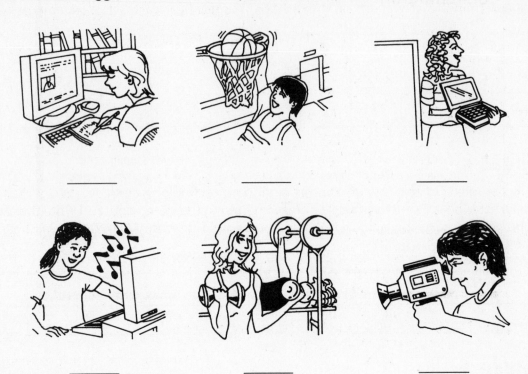

Actividad 9

Listen as two people discuss how the computer and the Internet have changed our lives. As you listen, organize their points into two columns by summarizing what they say. You will hear each set of statements twice.

1. _____   _____

2. _____   _____

3. _____   _____

4. _____   _____

Actividad 10

Read the following ad about a computer of the future. Then, answer the questions below.

CEREBRADOR: ¡EL FUTURO AHORA!

¿Está cansado de ver las computadoras del futuro en una película o de leer sobre ellas en una novela? ¿Quiere el futuro ahora? ¡Pues **Cerebrador** lo tiene!

♦ La información, los gráficos, la música en la Red...
   ¡todo sin límite!

♦ Grabar un disco, escribir un informe, navegar en la Red...
   ¡sólo hay que pensarlo y se logra en poco tiempo!

♦ ¿Tiene problemas de conexión o detesta sentarse a usar la computadora?
   Sólo necesita **Cerebrador** *y dos metros de espacio para poder ver todo en la pantalla: documentos, correo electrónico, su página Web, etc. Conecte a su propia cabeza.*

Con **Cerebrador** puede sacar fotos con una minicámara digital y crear diapositivas con ellas.

Llame ahora para pedir este fenómeno.

---

1. ¿Cómo se llama la computadora del anuncio?

_____

2. ¿Qué dice el anuncio que Ud. puede hacer con esta computadora?

_____

_____

_____

3. ¿Qué necesita para usar una computadora? ¿Es una computadora portátil?

_____

_____

_____

4. ¿Cree Ud. que es posible comprar una computadora como ésta? ¿Por qué?

_____

_____

_____

_____

Realidades 1

Capítulo 9B

Nombre _____

Hora _____

Fecha _____

WRITING

Actividad 11

Your favorite restaurant has great food, but the wait staff is always messing up the orders. Using the pictures as clues and the correct forms of the verbs **pedir** and **servir**, write what happens when the following people order their meals. Follow the model and remember to use the proper indirect object pronouns in your sentences.

| Modelo | Yo | El camarero |

Yo pido pescado pero el camarero me sirve pollo.
_____

1. Tú   Ellos

_____

2. Nosotros   La camarera

_____

3. María   Uds.

_____

4. Ellos   Nosotros

_____

5. Ramón y Yo   Los camareros

_____

Realidades 1

Capítulo 9B

Nombre _____

Fecha _____

Hora _____

WRITING

Actividad 12

Answer the following questions in 2–3 complete sentences using the verbs **saber** and/or **conocer**.

1. ¿Eres talentoso(a)? ¿Qué sabes hacer? ¿Tienes unos amigos muy talentosos? ¿Qué saben hacer ellos?

_____

_____

_____

_____

2. ¿Conoces a alguna persona famosa? ¿Quién? ¿Cómo es? ¿Alguien más en tu familia conoce a una persona famosa?

_____

_____

_____

_____

3. ¿Qué ciudades o países conocen tú y tu familia? ¿Cuándo los visitaste? ¿Qué lugares conocen tus amigos?

_____

_____

_____

_____

4. ¿Qué sabes de la geografía de Latinoamérica? (¿Sabes cuál es la capital de Uruguay? ¿Sabes cuántos países hay en Sudamérica?)

_____

_____

_____

_____

Realidades ①

Capítulo 9B

Nombre _____

Hora _____

Fecha _____

WRITING

Actividad 13

Describe the **cibercafé** below. First, tell three things that you can do there. Next, tell three items that they serve at the café, using the verb **servir** and the food items in the picture. Finally, tell what you can do if you need assistance at the **cibercafé**. Use the verb **pedir**, and the verbs **saber** and **conocer** to discuss how knowledgeable the staff is (**Ellos saben ayudar.../ Ellos conocen bien la Red...**).

Ud. puede _____

_____

_____

_____

Allí ellos _____

_____

_____

_____

_____

_____

_____

_____

_____

Song Lyrics

Track 01

ALEGRE VENGO

Alegre vengo de la montaña
De mi cabaña que alegre está
A mis amigos les traigo flores
De las mejores de mi rosal
A mis amigos les traigo flores
De las mejores de mi rosal

Ábreme la puerta
Ábreme la puerta
Que estoy en la calle
Y dirá la gente
Que esto es un desaire
Y dirá la gente
Que esto es un desaire

A la sarandela, a la sarandela
A la sarandela, de mi corazón
A la sarandela, a la sarandela
A la sarandela, de mi corazón

Allá dentro veo, allá dentro veo
Un bulto tapado
No sé si será un lechón asado
No sé si será un lechón asado
A la sarandela…

Track 02

LA MARIPOSA

La la la la laila laila laila
Bum bum bum bum bum

La la la la laila laila laila
Bum bum pata pata bum

Vamos todos a cantar,
vamos todos a bailar
la morenada.

Vamos todos a cantar,
vamos todos a bailar
la morenada.

Con los tacos,
con las manos.
¡Viva la fiesta!

Con los tacos,
con las manos.
¡Viva la fiesta!

Track 03

ERES TÚ

Como una promesa eres tú, eres tú
como una mañana de verano;
como una sonrisa eres tú, eres tú;
así, así eres tú.

Toda mi esperanza eres tú, eres tú,
como lluvia fresca en mis manos;
como fuerte brisa eres tú, eres tú;
así, así eres tú.

[estribillo]
Eres tú como el agua de mi fuente;
eres tú el fuego de mi hogar.
Eres tú como el fuego de mi hoguera;
eres tú el trigo de mi pan.

Como mi poema eres tú, eres tú;
como una guitarra en la noche.
Todo mi horizonte eres tú, eres tú;
así, así eres tú.

Eres tú como el agua de mi fuente;
eres tú el fuego de mi hogar.
Algo así eres tú;
algo así como el fuego de mi hoguera.
Algo así eres tú;
En mi vida algo así eres tú.

Eres tú como el fuego de mi hoguera;
eres tú el trigo de mi pan.
Algo así eres tú;
algo así como el fuego de mi hoguera.
Algo así eres tú…

Track 04

LA CUCARACHA

[estribillo]
La cucaracha, la cucaracha,
ya no quiere caminar,
porque no tiene, porque le falta
dinero para gastar.

La cucaracha, la cucaracha,
ya no quiere caminar,
porque no tiene, porque le falta
dinero para gastar.

Una cucaracha pinta
le dijo a una colorada:
Vámonos para mi tierra
a pasar la temporada.

Una cucaracha pinta
le dijo a una colorada:
Vámonos para mi tierra
a pasar la temporada.

La cucaracha, la cucaracha,
ya no quiere caminar,
porque no tiene, porque le falta
dinero para gastar.

Todas las muchachas tienen
en los ojos dos estrellas,
pero las mexicanitas
de seguro son más bellas.

Todas las muchachas tienen
en los ojos dos estrellas,
pero las mexicanitas
de seguro son más bellas.

La cucaracha, la cucaracha,
ya no quiere caminar,
porque no tiene, porque le falta
dinero para gastar.

Una cosa me da risa,
Pancho Villa sin camisa,
ya se van los carrancistas,
porque vienen los villistas.

Una cosa me da risa,
Pancho Villa sin camisa,
ya se van los carrancistas,
porque vienen los villistas.

La cucaracha, la cucaracha,
ya no quiere caminar,
porque no tiene, porque le falta
dinero para gastar.

Track 05

EL CÓNDOR PASA

Al cóndor de los Andes despertó
una luz,
una luz,
de un bello amanecer, amanecer.

Sus alas en lo alto extendió
y bajó,
y bajó,
al dulce manantial, para beber.

La nieve de las cumbres brilla ya
bajo el sol, el día y la luz.
La nieve de las cumbres brilla ya
bajo el sol, el día y la luz,
del bello amanecer, amanecer.

Al cóndor de los Andes despertó
una luz,
una luz,
de un bello amanecer, amanecer.

Sus alas en lo alto extendió
y bajó,
y bajó,
al dulce manantial, para beber.

La nieve de las cumbres brilla ya
bajo el sol, el día y la luz.
La nieve de las cumbres brilla ya
bajo el sol, el día y la luz,
del bello amanecer, amanecer.

Track 06

ASÓMATE AL BALCÓN

Asómate al balcón para que veas
mi parranda
Asómate al balcón para que veas quien
te canta
Asómate al balcón para que veas tus amigos
Asómate al balcón
Formemos un vacilón

Asómate, asómate, asómate, asómate

Yo sé que quieres dormir
Pero así es la Navidad
Y si tú no te levantas
Te sacamos de la cama
Aunque tengas que pelear

Asómate al balcón para (se repite)

¡Asómate, asómate, asómate, asómate!

Track 07

LA BAMBA

Para bailar la bamba, para bailar la bamba
se necesita una poca de gracia,
una poca de gracia y otra cosita
y arriba y arriba,
y arriba y arriba y arriba iré,
yo no soy marinero, yo no soy marinero,
por ti seré, por ti seré, por ti seré.

Bamba, bamba...

Una vez que te dije, una vez que te dije
que eras bonita, se te puso la cara,
se te puso la cara coloradita
y arriba y arriba,
y arriba y arriba y arriba iré,
yo no soy marinero, yo no soy marinero,
soy capitán, soy capitán, soy capitán.

Bamba, bamba...

Para subir al cielo, para subir al cielo
se necesita una escalera grande,
una escalera grande y otra chiquita
y arriba y arriba,
y arriba y arriba y arriba iré,
yo no soy marinero, yo no soy marinero,
por ti seré, por ti seré, por ti seré.

Bamba, bamba...

Track 08

HIMNO DEL ATHLÉTIC DE BILBAO

Tiene Bilbao un gran tesoro
que adora y mima con gran pasión.
Su club de fútbol
de bella historia,
lleno de gloria,
mil veces campeón.

Athlétic, Athlétic club
de limpia tradición,
ninguno más que tú
lleva mejor blasón.

Del fútbol eres rey,
te llaman el león
y la afición el rey
del fútbol español.

Cantemos pues los bilbainitos,
a nuestro club con gran amor,
para animarle con nuestro himno,
el canto digno del Alirón.

¡Alirón! ¡Alirón!
el Athlétic es campeón.

Track 9

PARA ROMPER LA PIÑATA

Echen confites y canelones
pa' los muchachos
que son comilones.
Castaña asada, piña cubierta,
pa' los muchachos que van a la puerta.

Ándale, Lola,
no te dilates
con la canasta
de los cacahuates.

En esta posada
nos hemos chasqueado,
porque la dueña
nada nos ha dado.

Track 10

PIÑATA

Dale, dale, dale,
no pierdas el tino,
porque si lo pierdes
pierdes el camino.

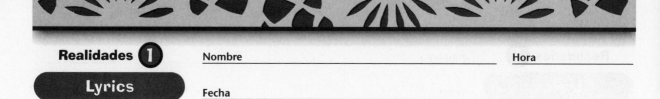

Track 11

LAS MAÑANITAS

Éstas son las mañanitas
que cantaba el Rey David,
pero no eran tan bonitas
como las cantan aquí.

[estribillo]
Despierta, mi bien, despierta,
mira que ya amaneció,
ya los pajarillos cantan,
la Luna ya se metió.

Despierta, mi bien, despierta,
mira que ya amaneció,
ya los pajarillos cantan,
la Luna ya se metió.

Si el sereno de la esquina
me quisiera hacer favor,
de apagar su linternita
mientras que pasa mi amor.

[estribillo]
Despierta, mi bien, despierta,
mira que ya amaneció,
ya los pajarillos cantan,
la Luna ya se metió.

Despierta, mi bien, despierta,
mira que ya amaneció,
ya los pajarillos cantan,
la Luna ya se metió.

Track 12

DE COLORES

De colores, de colores se visten los
campos en la primavera.
De colores, de colores son los pajaritos
que vienen de afuera.
De colores, de colores es el arco iris
que vemos salir.
Y por eso los grandes amores de
muchos colores me gustan a mí.
Y por eso los grandes amores de
muchos colores me gustan a mí.

De colores, de colores brillantes y finos
se viste la aurora.
De colores, de colores son los mil
reflejos que el sol atesora.
De colores, de colores se viste el
diamante que vemos lucir.
Y por eso los grandes amores de
muchos colores me gustan a mí.
Y por eso los grandes amores de
muchos colores me gustan a mí.

Track 13

MÉXICO LINDO Y QUERIDO

Voz de la guitarra mía,
al despertar la mañana,
quiere cantar su alegría
a mi tierra mexicana.

Yo le canto a tus volcanes,
a tus praderas y flores
que son como talismanes
del amor de mis amores.

México lindo y querido
si muero lejos de ti
que digan que estoy dormido
y que me traigan aquí.

México lindo y querido
si muero lejos de ti
que digan que estoy dormido
y que me traigan aquí.

Voz de la guitarra mía,
al despertar la mañana,
quiere cantar su alegría
a mi tierra mexicana.

Yo le canto a tus volcanes,
a tus praderas y flores
que son como talismanes
del amor de mis amores.

México lindo y querido
si muero lejos de ti
que digan que estoy dormido
y que me traigan aquí.

México lindo y querido
si muero lejos de ti
que digan que estoy dormido
y que me traigan aquí.

Track 14

MI CAFETAL

Porque la gente vive criticándome
paso la vida sin pensar en ná.

Porque la gente vive criticándome
paso la vida sin pensar en ná.

Pero no sabiendo que yo soy el hombre
que tengo un hermoso y lindo cafetal.

Pero no sabiendo que yo soy el hombre
que tengo un hermoso y lindo cafetal.

Yo tengo mi cafetal
y tú ya no tienes ná...

Yo tengo mi cafetal
y tú ya no tienes ná...

Colombia mi tierra bonita

Nada me importa que la gente diga
que no tengo plata que no tengo ná.

Nada me importa que la gente diga
que no tengo plata que no tengo ná.

Pero no sabiendo que yo soy el hombre
que tengo un hermoso y lindo cafetal.

Pero no sabiendo que yo soy el hombre
que tengo un hermoso y lindo cafetal.

Yo tengo mi cafetal
y tú ya no tienes ná...

Yo tengo mi cafetal
y tú ya no tienes ná...

Track 15

MARÍA ISABEL

La playa estaba desierta,
el mar bañaba tu piel,
cantando con mi guitarra
para ti, María Isabel.

La playa estaba desierta,
el mar bañaba tu piel,
cantando con mi guitarra
para ti, María Isabel.

[estribillo]
Toma tu sombrero y póntelo,
vamos a la playa, calienta el sol.

Toma tu sombrero y póntelo,
vamos a la playa, calienta el sol.

Chiri biri bi, poro, pom, pom.
Chiri biri bi, poro, pom, pom.
Chiri biri bi, poro, pom, pom.
Chiri biri bi, poro, pom, pom.

En la arena escribí tu nombre
y luego yo lo borré
para que nadie pisara
tu nombre: María Isabel.

En la arena escribí tu nombre
y luego yo lo borré
para que nadie pisara
tu nombre: María Isabel.

[estribillo]
Toma tu sombrero y póntelo,
vamos a la playa, calienta el sol.

Toma tu sombrero y póntelo,
vamos a la playa, calienta el sol.

Chiri biri bi, poro, pom, pom.
Chiri biri bi, poro, pom, pom.
Chiri biri bi, poro, pom, pom.
Chiri biri bi, poro, pom, pom.

La Luna fue caminando,
bajo las olas del mar;
tenía celos de tus ojos
y tu forma de mirar.

La Luna fue caminando,
bajo las olas del mar;
tenía celos de tus ojos
y tu forma de mirar.

[estribillo]
Toma tu sombrero y póntelo,
vamos a la playa, calienta el sol.

Toma tu sombrero y póntelo,
vamos a la playa, calienta el sol.

Chiri biri bi, poro, pom, pom.
Chiri biri bi, poro, pom, pom.
Chiri biri bi, poro, pom, pom.
Chiri biri bi, poro, pom, pom.

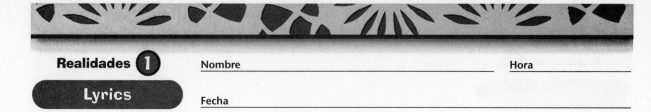

Track 16

LA GOLONDRINA

¿Adónde irá veloz y fatigada,
la golondrina que de aquí se irá?
Allí en el cielo se mirará angustiada,
sin paz ni abrigo que dio mi amor.

Junto a mi pecho allí hará su nido,
en donde pueda la estación pasar.
También yo estoy en la región perdida
haciendo salto y sin poder volar.

También yo estoy en la región perdida
haciendo salto y sin poder volar.

Junto a mi pecho allí hará su nido,
en donde pueda la estación pasar.
También yo estoy en la región perdida
haciendo salto y sin poder volar.

Track 17

¡VIVA JUJUY!

Vamos con ese bailecito

Adentrito cholo

¡Viva Jujuy!
¡Viva la Puna!
¡Viva mi amada!
¡Vivan los cerros
pintarrajeados
de mi quebrada...!

¡Viva Jujuy!
¡Viva la Puna!
¡Viva mi amada!
¡Vivan los cerros
pintarrajeados
de mi quebrada...!

De mi quebrada
humahuaqueña...

No te separes
de mis amores,
¡tú eres mi dueña!

La, lara, rara, rara

No te separes
de mis amores,
¡tú eres mi dueña!

Dos, dos y se va la otrita

Adentro

Viva Jujuy
y la hermosura
de las jujeñas!
Vivan las trenzas
bien renegridas
de mi morena!

Viva Jujuy
y la hermosura
de las jujeñas!
Vivan las trenzas
bien renegridas
de mi morena!

De mi morena
mal pagadora

No te separes
de mis amores
¡tú eres mi dueña!

La, lara, rara, rara

No te separes
de mis amores
¡tú eres mi dueña!

Track 18

ADIÓS MUCHACHOS

Adiós muchachos, compañeros de mi vida,
barra querida de aquellos tiempos.
Me toca a mí hoy emprender la retirada,
debo alejarme de mi buena muchachada.

Adiós, muchachos,
ya me voy y me resigno,
contra el destino nadie la talla.
Se terminaron para mí todas las farras.
Mi cuerpo enfermo no resiste más.

Dos lágrimas sinceras
derramo en mi partida
por la barra querida
que nunca me olvidó.
Y al darle a mis amigos
mi adiós postrero
les doy con toda el alma
mi bendición.

Adiós muchachos, compañeros de mi vida,
barra querida de aquellos tiempos.
Me toca a mí hoy emprender la retirada,
debo alejarme de mi buena muchachada.

Adiós, muchachos,
ya me voy y me resigno,
contra el destino nadie la talla.
Se terminaron para mí todas las farras.
Mi cuerpo enfermo no resiste más.